INCORPORATION AND BUSINESS GUIDE
FOR BRITISH COLUMBIA

D1616675

DATE DUE

BRODART   Cat. No. 23-221

INCORPORATION AND BUSINESS GUIDE
FOR BRITISH COLUMBIA

Janice Mucalov, BA(HONS), LLB

Self-Counsel Press
(a division of)
International Self-Counsel Press Ltd.
Canada   USA

Self-Counsel Press acknowledges the financial support of the Government of Canada through the Book Publishing Industry Development Program (BPIDP) for our publishing activities.

Printed in Canada.

First edition: 1971
Tenth edition: 1983
Fifteenth edition: 1990
Twentieth edition: 2000; 2001

Canadian Cataloguing in Publication Data

Mucalov, Janice I. (Janice Irene), 1955-
Incorporation and business guide for British Columbia

    (Self-counsel legal series)
    First-3rd eds. by Christopher L. Pocock; 4th-19th eds. by J.D. James;
    1st-4th eds. have title: B.C. incorporation guide;
    5th-6th eds. have title: B.C. incorporation and business guide.
    ISBN 1-55180-301-1

1. Incorporation — British Columbia — Popular works. 2. Private companies —
British Columbia — Popular works. I. Title. II. Series.
KEB316.Z82J35 2000   346.711'06622   C00-910268-X
KF1420.Z9J35 2000

Self-Counsel Press
(a division of)
International Self-Counsel Press Ltd.

1481 Charlotte Road	1704 N. State Street
North Vancouver, BC V7J lHl	Bellingham, WA 98225
Canada	USA

CONTENTS

TABLES

SAMPLES

INCORPORATION SERVICES
AVAILABLE FROM THE PUBLISHER

To incorporate your company, you will need to file certain forms. You may type these yourself, but it is easier and quicker to used preprinted forms, or, if you wish, you can take advantage of our typing service and have all the forms typed out for you. **Note:** if you use the typing service, you do not need to purchase the preprinted forms.

Typing service

If you have decided to incorporate in British Columbia, why not use Self-Counsel's convenient typing service and have all the forms typed out for you? The service covers the cost of the preprinted forms and the typing out of these forms according to information that you provide. We do not file the documents for you, nor does the typing service fee cover your filing fees.

Cost: $125 plus GST

If you have decided to incorporate a small, non-distributing company, here's how we can help you:

1. Read this book carefully before contacting us. Call (604) 986-3366 or 1-800-663-3007 between 8:30 a.m. and 5:00 p.m. and we will mail or fax the data sheets to you. Or, download the data sheets from our Web site at <www.self-counsel.com>.

2. Reserve the name you have chosen with the Registrar of Companies.

3. Use the *Incorporation and Business Guide* as a reference to complete the data sheets, and then mail, fax, or e-mail the sheets back to us, together with your cheque, money order, or Master-Card/Visa number.

    Mail to: Self-Counsel Press   Fax to: (604) 986-3947
              1481 Charlotte Road   E-mail to: incorp@self-counsel.com
              North Vancouver, BC V7J 1H1

4. When we receive your data sheets, we will type up the documents and return them to you for filing with the Registrar of Companies.

Please note that, while your documents will be completed by competent personnel, we cannot and do not give legal advice. If you have complicated tax or legal problems with incorporation, you should see a lawyer.

Preprinted forms

Self-Counsel's preprinted *Incorporation Forms and Disk* kit contains copies of the forms you will need for a simple incorporation in British Columbia. The kit contains:

*   2 copies of the memorandum of incorporation
*   2 copies of the articles of incorporation
*   2 notices of registered and records office
*   2 consent resolutions of subscribers and first directors
*   4 share certificates

Along with the preprinted forms, the kit also includes a PC 3½" disk which contains electronic versions of the forms in Word 6.0 and pdf format.

The forms are designed to be used in conjunction with this book. Read them carefully and complete them by following the instructions and samples in this book.

Cost: $23.95

If you are unable to purchase the forms at the store where you purchased this book, complete and mail the order form.

✂ --

ORDER FORM

Please send me the following items prepaid:

Item	Quantity	Unit Price	Total
Company Act	_____	$18.50	_____
Incorporation Forms for BC (kit)*	_____	$23.95	_____
Minute book*	_____	$22.95	_____
Extra share certificates*	_____	$ 0.50 each	_____

SEALS AND STAMPS

Seals and stamps are not shipped from Self-Counsel Press. They are shipped directly from the manufacturer.

Seal, up to 39 characters (include spaces)*	_____	$45.95	_____
Seal, 40 or more characters (include spaces)*	_____	$55.95	_____
Deposit stamp (with 2 lines)*	_____	$16.95	_____
Endorsement stamp*	_____	$12.95	_____
Name and address stamp (with 3 lines)*	_____	$16.95	_____
Subtotal			_____
***Add PST to items marked with ***			_____
Add 7% GST calculated on Subtotal			_____
Postage & handling books, kits, etc. (includes GST)		$3.50	_____
Postage & handling seals & stamps (includes GST)		$5.00	_____
TOTAL			_____

All prices subject to change without notice.

Please send the items checked above to:

Mr./Ms. _____

Address _____City_____

Province_____Postal code _____Telephone _____

Name of corporation _____

Corporation address (for stamp) if not same as above _____

Please charge my   ❑ Visa   ❑ MasterCard

MasterCard/Visa number _____

Expiry date _____

Signature _____

Please check your seals and stamps upon receipt.
We will not be responsible for errors reported more than 30 days after mailing.

PREFACE

Why are you interested in incorporating? Probably because of your accountant's suggestion or because you have heard vague references from your friends and business associates about the advantages of having a company or maybe because you just think it's the thing to do.

Whatever your reason, you are probably confused and perhaps even frustrated at the idea of having to spend hundreds of dollars for something you know nothing about, especially when you are having trouble seeing the benefits that are supposed to accrue to you.

If so, this book is for you. For a relatively small investment, this publication will clear away those uncertainties and explain in simple, layperson's language the whys and wherefores of incorporating and, in addition, may save you hundreds of dollars in lawyer's fees.

However, there are some areas where this book cannot replace your lawyer or accountant. Specifically, if you are setting up a business where there are opposing interests, or if you are involved in intricate and complex debt or share issues, it is essential that proper counsel be retained.

If you are not involved in such a situation and you choose to do your own incorporation, by following the procedures set out in this manual, you will save a substantial amount ($100 to $600) in legal fees for incorporating a company.

In any event, if the business is successful, whether you seek competent professional help prior to incorporation or not, you will undoubtedly require the services of a qualified accountant following incorporation. Doing the books yourself is both dangerous and, in the long run, expensive.

This publication is not meant to circumvent or to derogate from the value of professional help. It is meant as an aid to persons who desire a simple incorporation and find that the money spent for professional fees may be better spent elsewhere, or for those who simply want to become acquainted with the legal and practical implications of a limited company.

— Editors,
Self-Counsel Press

NOTICE TO READERS

ACKNOWLEDGMENTS

I am very grateful to the chartered accountants and management consulting firm of Grant Thornton. In particular, I'd like to thank both Philip Noble, CA, and Kam Sandhu, CA, of Grant Thornton, who provided the information on taxes and financial statements for this book.

1
INTRODUCTION TO THE INCORPORATED BUSINESS

You are probably engaged in a small business or are thinking about starting one, either by yourself or with someone else. One of the first decisions you'll have to make is what kind of business "vehicle" you should choose. In Canada, there are only three ways to carry on any business: through a sole proprietorship, a partnership, or a limited company. These encompass every type of business, from the smallest corner grocery store to General Motors of Canada Limited.

If you are already carrying on business and are not incorporated, you must be operating either as a sole proprietor or as a partner in a business. There are also special entities such as organizations engaged in charitable or semi-charitable enterprises, but these do not concern us here and will not be discussed. For information on incorporating a non-profit organization, see *The Nonprofit Organization Guide,* another title in the Self-Counsel Series.

1. THE SOLE PROPRIETORSHIP AND THE PARTNERSHIP

The simplest and most inexpensive legal form of carrying on any business is by registering a proprietorship (where only one person is involved) or a partnership (where two or more people are involved).

Sole proprietorships and partnerships must be registered in Victoria, but the cost is modest and the procedure is simple. All you need to do is select a name that is unique and cannot be confused with that of another business operating in your area and write to the Registrar of Companies in Victoria to reserve your name. Be sure to include the appropriate fee. The Registrar will conduct a name search and send you a one-page Declaration form to fill out. For current fees, contact the Registrar of Companies at (250) 387-7848 or check the Ministry of Finance and Corporate Relations' Web site at <www.gov.bc.ca/fin/>.

In addition, sole proprietorships indicating a number of names to denote a partnership must also be registered under the Partnership Act. (See Sample 1 for a Declaration for Registration of Sole Proprietorship and Sample 2 for a Declaration for Registration of Partnership.)

Aside from the simplicity, the major advantage of a proprietorship or partnership is that, if you expect your business to incur losses for some time and you continue to hold down another job, you can offset all the losses in the business against your employment income. This is particularly advantageous in a husband-wife business where both spouses have outside sources of income.

However, there are some drawbacks to a partnership or a proprietorship. First, if you are involved in a partnership, you incur the cost of a partnership agreement. This agreement regulates the conduct of the partners. Without it, you leave yourself wide open to problems down the road. The cost of a properly prepared agreement can be $300 or more.

Second, a proprietorship or partnership is not recognized in law as a separate legal entity. Therefore, all debts and liabilities

SAMPLE 1
DECLARATION FOR REGISTRATION OF SOLE PROPRIETORSHIP

BRITISH COLUMBIA

Ministry of Finance
and Corporate Relations
Corporate and Personal
Property Registries

Mailing Address:
PO Box 9431 Stn Prov Govt
Victoria BC V8W 9V3
Location:
2nd Floor – 940 Blanshard Street
Victoria BC

**DECLARATION FOR REGISTRATION
OF GENERAL PARTNERSHIP
OR SOLE PROPRIETORSHIP**

CORPORATE REGISTRY

GOVERNMENT AGENT

REGISTRATION NO.

Phone: (250) 356-2893 or
775-1044 (Greater Vancouver only).

NAME APPROVAL NO. – *If known*

N R

A. Name and Return Mailing Address for this Document

NAME	John James Doe
ADDRESS	555 Yang Street
CITY/ PROVINCE/ POSTAL CODE	Vancouver, BC Z1P 0G0

Note: The registration of a business name under the *Partnership Act* does not provide any protection for that name.

Please **TYPE** or **PRINT CLEARLY**. Press firmly – you are making three copies.

B. Business Information – *This section must be completed by everyone.*

BUSINESS NAME

Green's Office Supplies

BUSINESS ADDRESS – *Must be the physical location of the business in BC*, not just a general delivery, post office box, rural route, site, or comp. number

STREET	CITY	PROVINCE	POSTAL CODE
555 Yang Street, Vancouver		**British Columbia**	Z1P 0G0

MAILING ADDRESS – *Complete only if different from Business Address*

STREET	CITY	PROVINCE	POSTAL CODE

START DATE OF BUSINESS IN BRITISH COLUMBIA	DESCRIBE NATURE OF BUSINESS (e.g., grocery store, manufacturing)
YYYY MM DD 2000 01 15	Office supplier

C. Proprietorship – *I hereby certify that no other person is associated with me in this proprietorship.*

PROPRIETOR NAME – *State owner's name*	SIGNATURE
John James Doe	X *J J Doe*

RESIDENTIAL OR REGISTERED ADDRESS – *Must be a physical location*, CANNOT be just a general delivery, post office box, rural route, site, or comp. number

555 Yang Street, Vancouver BC Z1P 0G0

D. Partnership – *We hereby certify that the persons named in Section D are the only members of this partnership.*

PARTNER NAME	RESIDENTIAL OR REGISTERED ADDRESS – *Must be a physical location*, CANNOT be just a general delivery, post office box, rural route, site, or comp. number
SIGNATURE X	
PARTNER NAME	RESIDENTIAL OR REGISTERED ADDRESS – *Must be a physical location*, CANNOT be just a general delivery, post office box, rural route, site, or comp. number
SIGNATURE X	
PARTNER NAME	RESIDENTIAL OR REGISTERED ADDRESS – *Must be a physical location*, CANNOT be just a general delivery, post office box, rural route, site, or comp. number
SIGNATURE X	

FIN 707 Rev. 1999 / 5 / 10   **WHITE/CANARY:** REGISTRAR OF COMPANIES **PINK:** APPLICANT

SAMPLE 2
DECLARATION FOR REGISTRATION OF PARTNERSHIP

BRITISH COLUMBIA

Ministry of Finance and Corporate Relations
Corporate and Personal Property Registries

Mailing Address:
PO Box 9431 Stn Prov Govt
Victoria BC V8W 9V3
Location:
2nd Floor – 940 Blanshard Street
Victoria BC

Phone: (250) 356-2893 or
775-1044 (Greater Vancouver only).

NAME APPROVAL NO. – *If known*

N R | | | | | | |

DECLARATION FOR REGISTRATION OF GENERAL PARTNERSHIP OR SOLE PROPRIETORSHIP

CORPORATE REGISTRY

GOVERNMENT AGENT

REGISTRATION NO.

A. Name and Return Mailing Address for this Document

NAME	John Dean Doe
ADDRESS	321 Yin Street
CITY/ PROVINCE/ POSTAL CODE	Vancouver, BC Z1P 0G0

Note: The registration of a business name under the *Partnership Act* does not provide any protection for that name.

Please **TYPE** or **PRINT CLEARLY**. Press firmly – you are making three copies.

B. Business Information – *This section must be completed by everyone.*

BUSINESS NAME

J & J Groceries

BUSINESS ADDRESS – **Must be the physical location of the business in BC,** *not just a general delivery, post office box, rural route, site, or comp. number*

STREET	CITY	PROVINCE	POSTAL CODE
123 Any Street, North Vancouver		British Columbia	Z1P 0G0

MAILING ADDRESS – *Complete only if different from Business Address*

STREET	CITY	PROVINCE	POSTAL CODE

START DATE OF BUSINESS IN BRITISH COLUMBIA			DESCRIBE NATURE OF BUSINESS (e.g., grocery store, manufacturing)
YYYY	MM	DD	
2 0 0 0	0 1	1 5	Retail Grocers

C. Proprietorship – *I hereby certify that no other person is associated with me in this proprietorship.*

PROPRIETOR NAME – *State owner's name*	SIGNATURE
	X

RESIDENTIAL OR REGISTERED ADDRESS – **Must be a physical location,** *CANNOT be just a general delivery, post office box, rural route, site, or comp. number*

D. Partnership – *We hereby certify that the persons named in Section D are the only members of this partnership.*

PARTNER NAME	RESIDENTIAL OR REGISTERED ADDRESS – **Must be a physical location,** *CANNOT be just a general delivery, post office box, rural route, site, or comp. number*
John Dean Doe	321 Yin Street, Vancouver BC Z1P 1G0
SIGNATURE X *J D Doe*	
PARTNER NAME	RESIDENTIAL OR REGISTERED ADDRESS – **Must be a physical location,** *CANNOT be just a general delivery, post office box, rural route, site, or comp. number*
Jean Jane Doe	321 Yin Street, Vancouver BC Z1P 1G0
SIGNATURE X *J J Doe*	
PARTNER NAME	RESIDENTIAL OR REGISTERED ADDRESS – **Must be a physical location,** *CANNOT be just a general delivery, post office box, rural route, site, or comp. number*
SIGNATURE X	

FIN 707 Rev. 1999 / 5 / 10   **WHITE/CANARY:** REGISTRAR OF COMPANIES   **PINK:** APPLICANT

incurred by the business become the personal responsibility of the proprietor or the partners. This means that all your personal assets are at risk, including your house and personal savings.

In addition, partners are fully liable, jointly and individually, for debts incurred by each other while acting in the course of business, regardless of the proportionate capital contribution of the individual parties. And be warned — you may be considered to be in partnership with someone even though you haven't filed a formal Declaration of Partnership form at the office of the Registrar of Companies in Victoria. This is because, legally, a partnership is created by the relationship of the parties and not by any formal act or documents signed by the parties. There is no established test as to what constitutes a partnership, although the following questions offer some guidelines:

(a) Is there a sharing of net profits and losses?

(b) Do any of the parties act as agents for the others?

(c) Is there any property held in joint tenancy?

(d) Is there any implication of partnership on your firm's letterhead or in its correspondence?

(e) Is the nature of the work relationship that of a partnership?

2. CORPORATIONS

Many people prefer to carry on business as a corporation because of the unique characteristics of a corporate entity. A corporation is a distinct legal entity, an "artificial person" quite separate from the people who are its shareholders. When you incorporate, you actually create a new person in the eyes of the law. The assets and debts of a corporation belong to it — not to the individual shareholders.

2.1 Advantages to incorporating

Because of the characteristics outlined above, there are four major advantages for people who incorporate their businesses.

2.1.a Greater source of capital

There is potentially a greater source of capital available in an incorporation than in a partnership or proprietorship. Since the company is an entity separate from its shareholders, people may invest money in it without accepting any further responsibility for conducting the company business and without worrying about becoming liable for the debts of the company.

2.1.b Perpetual existence

Since the company is a separate entity, it does not expire when the shareholders die. Substantial estate planning benefits result from this aspect of incorporation.

2.1.c Limited liability

Limited liability is the main reason businesses incorporate. The most advantageous and unique characteristic of a company is its limited liability, and this is why corporations are referred to as "limited companies." The words "Limited" or "Ltd.," "Incorporated" or "Inc.," "Corporation" or "Corp." must appear in the names of all companies and must *not* appear in the name of a proprietorship or partnership. This very special concept is contained in section 55(3) of the Company Act, which simply states:

> No member of a company is personally liable for the debts, obligations, or acts of the company.

This means that your liability as a shareholder is limited to the amount of money you owe the company (i.e., for shares), and doesn't include the amounts of money that the company itself owes to its creditors. This is obviously an important advantage.

There are, however, certain limitations to the limited liability of a company, the most important being that, in many instances, creditors, particularly banks, will not extend credit to a small company without your personal guarantee as its shareholder. (A bank may also require the corporation's owners to take out life insurance as a condition to obtaining a loan. The type of insurance involved is almost always term insurance, but the important point to remember is that the premium on this type of transaction is a *company* expense. If you have paid for this personally, you are entitled to be reimbursed by the company.)

However, if you don't personally guarantee your company's loans, your liability as a shareholder is limited to what you have invested in the company and the amount you owe for unpaid shares, if any. The following examples illustrate these principles.

Example 1

John Doe and Jack Doe carry on business as a partnership known as J & J Industries.

J & J Industries incurs debts of $25 000.

The assets of J & J Industries are $10 000.

A creditor successfully petitions J & J Industries into bankruptcy or simply gets a judgement against J & J Industries.

All the assets of John Doe and Jack Doe, as individuals, including possibly their homes and cars, may be executed against to repay the $15 000 debt incurred by the partnership over and above its assets.

Example 2

John Doe and Jack Doe carry on business as a corporation known as J & J Industries

Limited, with John Doe and Jack Doe the only shareholders, each having purchased one share at $1 (although any number of shares can be purchased).

J & J Industries Limited incurs debts of $25 000.

The assets of J & J Industries Limited are considered to have a market value of $10 000.

A creditor successfully petitions J & J Industries Limited into bankruptcy.

The creditors can realize $10 000 on the assets of the company, but they have no rights against John and Jack as individuals,* regardless of the value of personal assets that John and Jack may own outside the company.

The creditors are creditors of the company, not of John and Jack.

2.1.d Community recognition

An incorporated company usually has more credibility in the eyes of banks, creditors, and customers than a sole proprietorship or a partnership. If you've gone to the trouble and expense of incorporating, indicating that you have long-range plans for your business, you are taken more seriously.

2.1.e Tax advantages

The potential tax advantages of incorporating are so important that a whole chapter has been devoted to the subject (see chapter 2).

2.2 Disadvantages to incorporating

There are, however, disadvantages to incorporating that you should consider. First, operating through a company does entail extra paperwork. You have to file incorporation documents, notices, and annual reports. You have to file two tax returns: one for your company and one for yourself.

---

*The general exception to this rule is that, as directors of a company, Jack and John remain personally liable for the debts of the company as they relate to wages and commissions owed to employees.

You must maintain proper accounting records. Section 171 of the Company Act, the act that regulates corporations, states:

Accounting records required.

171. (1) Every company must keep proper accounting records in respect of all financial and other transactions of the company, and, without limiting the generality of the foregoing, must keep records of

(a) every sum of money received and disbursed by the company and the matters in respect of which the receipt and disbursement takes place,

(b) every sale and purchase by the company,

(c) asset and liability of the company, and

(d) every other transaction affecting the financial position of the company.

(2) The accounting records of a company must be kept at a place determined by the directors, but the Registrar may order that they be kept in British Columbia.

(3) The accounting records of a company must be open to the inspection of any director during the normal business hours of the company.

(4) Subject to the articles or an ordinary resolution, the directors may determine to what extent, at which times and places and under what conditions the accounting records of the company must be open to the inspection of members.

(5) Every company that contravenes a requirement of this section commits an offence.

There may also be additional government paperwork to do from time to time.

Also, there is the cost of setting up and maintaining a minute book and records office (see chapter 5) and your duties as a director (see chapter 12).

Second, if the company has an income of more than $200 000 per year, you actually pay significantly higher taxes than if you weren't incorporated. However, I assume this situation applies to so few companies that further comment is unnecessary.

Third, there is the cost and bother of doing the incorporating. By the time you are finished, you will have spent $300 to $400 and a few hours of your time.

3. SUMMARY OF WAYS OF CARRYING ON BUSINESS

As discussed above, there are three main legal forms an organization can take. These forms and their characteristics are outlined briefly below for quick reference.

Proprietorship

(a) Unincorporated

(b) Owned by one person

(c) Creditors have a legal claim on both the investment in the business and the personal assets of the owner

Partnership

(a) Unincorporated

(b) Each partner has unlimited liability in a general partnership arrangement

(c) The acts of one partner in the course of the management of the business are binding upon the other partners

(d) The partnership dissolves upon the death or withdrawal of any partner, or upon the acceptance of a new partner

J & J INDUSTRIES LIMITED

March 31, 200-

Current Assets

Cash	$ 20 000
Accounts receivable	290 000
Inventories	90 000
TOTAL	$400 000

Current Liabilities

Trade payables	$100 000
Wages payable	10 000
Current portion of long term debt	90 000
TOTAL	$200 000

Incorporated company

(a) Incorporated in most provinces by Memorandum of Association or federally by Articles of Incorporation

(b) Exists as a separate legal entity

(c) Shareholders are liable only to the extent of their investment and callable shares they hold in the corporation (callable shares are those that are not fully paid for)

(d) Usually possesses tax advantages

4. FINANCIAL STATEMENTS AND THEIR IMPORTANCE

No matter what legal form an organization takes, the preparation of meaningful financial statements is vital because various people will have an interest in the financial affairs of the organization, namely, owners, managers, creditors, the Canada Customs and Revenue Agency (formerly Revenue Canada), and prospective buyers.

To illustrate, let's assume that you're a bank manager and that J & J Industries Limited, a medium-sized corporation in the business of manufacturing, approaches you for a $10 000 loan. The principals explain that the funds are necessary for plant expansion. As a prospective creditor, you would be interested in two things: the ability of J & J Industries Limited to pay the regular installments of principal and interest on the loan and the amount the bank would recover if the company couldn't meet its obligation.

To satisfy your curiosity, you would have to examine the financial statements of the company. The annual income would be shown on the profit and loss, or income and expense, statement. This figure, if compared with the income statement from prior periods, would indicate to you the rate of financial growth of the enterprise.

In addition, you'd be able to determine whether or not enough total revenue is generated to repay the proposed loan. The balance sheet of the company would indicate any other long-term debt for which the company is liable. Furthermore, you could determine which assets (inventories, accounts receivable, etc.) may be available as security for the proposed loan.

The company's ability to pay its current obligations is another important indicator of the financial health of the enterprise. This ability to pay present debts when due can also be determined from the balance sheet. This indicator is expressed as a ratio (called the "current ratio") and is calculated by dividing the total current assets by the total current liabilities. This is shown in Sample 3. Current assets exceed current liabilities in the ratio of 2:1. In other words, the working capital position of the company in this case is healthy.

In summary, by looking at the financial statements of J & J Industries Limited, you would obtain much of the information so vital to your decision regarding the loan.

The preceding illustration shows how financial statements can be useful to potential creditors. Further, financial statements are useful to anyone who has an interest (monetary or otherwise) in an enterprise. Just as certain medical implements are the tools by which a doctor can get some indication of physical health, so financial statements are the tools by which interested parties can measure the financial health of an organization.

Below is a breakdown, in point form, of the three major financial statements: the balance sheet, the profit and loss statement, and the statement of retained earnings. They're discussed here to give you some idea of the function and contents of financial statements.

4.1 Balance sheet

The balance sheet is a position statement, not a historical record; it shows what is owed at a given date. There are three sections to a balance sheet: assets, liabilities,

and statement of retained earnings (see Sample 4).

4.1.a Assets

Current assets are those assets that will be used up within one year of the current balance sheet date. Normal carrying value of such assets is at original cost or market value, whichever is lower.

Fixed assets are those assets that provide benefits to the organization over a longer period than one year from the current balance sheet date. Carrying value is generally at original cost less accumulated depreciation. The amount of depreciation is based on the length of the useful life of the asset and the original cost of the asset.

To illustrate:

Building: original cost $40 000

Useful life: 20 years

Portion of asset cost which expires in each period:

$$\frac{\$40\ 000}{20} = \$2\ 000$$

This type of depreciation is normally calculated on a reducing balance basis, but for this illustration I have used the straight-line method. The sum of $2 000 is charged to the profit and loss statement in each period and is accumulated on the balance sheet as a reduction of the original cost of the asset. Thus, five years after the building was bought, the balance sheet would show:

Building, at cost	$40 000
Less accumulated depreciation	
(5 x 2 000)	$10 000
Book value of building	$30 000

Because the asset may be sold for more than the original cost, the book value doesn't necessarily indicate the amount the equity holders should receive for their ownership of the building. (**Note:** The "equity holders" in a company are the shareholders.)

BALANCE SHEET FOR UNINCORPORATED BUSINESS

ASSETS

Current Assets

Cash on hand and in bank		$720.12	
Accounts receivable less allowance for doubtful accounts		657.72	
Merchandise inventory valued at the lower of original cost or market		3 212.63	
Prepaid expenses		157.55	
Total current assets			$ 4 748.02

Fixed Asset — At Cost

Land		$2 320.00	
Building	$5 767.16		
Less: accumulated depreciation	1 727.92	4 039.24	
Store fixtures	3 726.12		
Less: accumulated depreciation	982.36	2 743.76	
Delivery truck	2 760.20		
Less: accumulated depreciation	513.60	2 246.60	11 349.60
			$16 097.62

LIABILITIES & PARTNERS' EQUITY

Current Liabilities

Trade Accounts payable		$2 772.58	
Accrued wage		75.20	
Employees' income tax payable		60.16	
Accrued real estate taxes		220.00	
Total current liabilities			$3 127.54

Retained Earnings and Partners' Equity*

Jones's share	$6 484.84		
Smith's share	6 484.84		
			12 969.68
			$16 097.62

*If the company was incorporated, this would read as follows:

Issued and fully paid for:

Jones — 50 shares at $1.00 = $50.00

Smith — 50 shares at $1.00 = $50.00

CAPITAL STOCK

Common stock, no par value — 100 shares.

Retained earnings $12 969.68

4.1.b Liabilities and owners' equity

Liabilities are those things that the company owes to others, on both a short-term and a long-term basis, and include such things as accounts payable, bank loans, and unpaid taxes.

Owners' equity is determined by subtracting liabilities from total assets and represents the carrying value of the owners' shareholding for accounting purposes. This value may very well be different from the fair market value of the owners' shareholdings because fair market value can only be determined from what an arm's length purchaser would be prepared to pay for the shareholdings, and not necessarily what the shareholdings are carried at for accounting purposes.

4.2 Profit and loss statement

The profit and loss statement indicates the company's profit or loss by subtracting the total expenses for that period from the total revenue for that period. There are two ways of determining when revenue is earned and when expenses are incurred: the cash basis method and the accrual basis method.

In the *cash basis* method no revenue is recognized until cash is received. No expenses are recognized until cash is disbursed. If, on the other hand, accounting is done on the *accrual basis*, revenue is recognized as soon as it is earned. Expenses are recognized as soon as they are incurred. The actual receipt or disbursement of cash is irrelevant.

4.3 Statement of retained earnings

The statement of retained earnings is a statement showing accumulated retained earnings from year to year. Added to the opening balance of retained earnings for the year is the current year's net profit (after income taxes are paid). From that sum, dividends declared and paid are subtracted to arrive at a closing balance for the current year.

The closing balance is summarized on the balance sheet in Sample 4 as the entry Retained Earnings and Partners' Equity. The closing balance for the current year becomes the opening balance for the following year.

5. ONE-STOP BUSINESS REGISTRATION

To help small-business operators complete some of the most common documents required to start up and operate their businesses, the provincial government has created One-Stop Business Registration (OSBR). It is an easy-to-use, interactive computer program that takes from 20 minutes to one hour to complete.

At an OSBR computer workstation, you can apply for any or all of the following five registrations:

- Declaration for Proprietorship or Partnership (Name Registration) (BC Registrar of Companies)

- Application for Registration as a Vendor (Provincial Sales Tax) (BC Consumer Taxation Branch)

- Employer's Registration Application (Workers' Compensation Board)

- Personal Optional Protection Insurance Application (Workers' Compensation Board)

- Business Number Accounts: GST, corporate income tax, payroll deductions, and import/export (CCRA [formerly Revenue Canada])

Note: See Chapter 6 for more information on the last four of the above five registrations.

You can personally choose the application forms you wish to complete, or the OSBR program can help you determine which registrations are required. OSBR then sends the results to the various agencies and prints out copies for you.

OSBR is currently available at OSBR computer workstations in over 30 locations in Vancouver (at the Canada/British Columbia Business Service Centre — see section **6.** below), Victoria, and elsewhere across the province. Call Enquiry BC's toll-free number at 1-800-663-7867 or check <www.osbr.sb.gov.bc.ca> for the location nearest you.

6.   CANADA/BRITISH COLUMBIA BUSINESS SERVICE CENTRE

The Canada/British Columbia Business Service Centre is a joint federal and provincial "one-stop shop" where you can get information about how to start and operate a business, taxation, regulations, and legal requirements. Located in Vancouver, the centre is open from 8:30 a.m. to 4:30 p.m., Monday through Friday. It is staffed by business service officers who can assist you with your inquiries in person or by telephone. The address and telephone number are:

Canada/British Columbia
Business Service Centre
601 West Cordova Street
Vancouver, BC V6B 1G1
Telephone: (604) 775-5520 or
          1-800-667-2272

In addition, the centre operates a 24-hour, toll-free automated fax service. Phone (604) 775-5515 in Vancouver or 1-800-667-2272 in BC. The system allows you to request documents on topics such as taxation, CPP deductions, and GST returns, which are faxed to you free within minutes of your call.

The centre has also posted dozens of documents on the Internet with excellent information on planning, starting, financing, marketing, and operating your small business. See <www.sb.gov.bc.ca>.

2
LIMIT YOURSELF TO LIMIT TAXES

There can be substantial tax advantages to incorporating your business. This section outlines the major ones.

1. BASIC CORPORATE RATE*

In British Columbia, the basic combined federal and provincial corporate income tax rate (before the small-business deduction and manufacturing and processing credit — see section **2.** below) is approximately 46%.

2. QUALIFYING FOR THE SMALL-BUSINESS TAX RATE

If your business qualifies for the small-business rate, you can receive a substantial reduction in taxes payable on business earnings. The rate for the first $200 000 of all net income from active business is about 19%.

To qualify for the small-business rate on the first $200 000 of net, certain conditions must be met:

(a) Your company must be a Canadian-controlled private corporation. This means that it must be a private Canadian corporation that is not controlled directly or indirectly by one or more non-residents, or by one or more public corporations, or by any such combination.

(b) Your company must generate income from an active business in Canada.

(c) If your company is "associated" with other corporations, they all must share the small-business tax rate on the first $200 000 of combined active business income.

If the corporation fails any of these three conditions, then the tax rate will be between about 39% and 46%, depending on whether or not the income is from manufacturing and processing.

Any business carried on by your company will be considered active with the following two exceptions:

(a) Personal services businesses (personal services that would ordinarily be provided by an individual employee rather than by a company)

(b) Investment businesses

Personal services corporations are held ineligible in order to prevent an individual who incorporates to obtain the benefit of lower taxes when, in fact, he or she could be considered an "employee" of the company paying remuneration. This type of corporation usually has income from one main source and has less than five employees. If you're contemplating forming a personal services corporation, you should obtain professional advice.

Personal services businesses and investment businesses will be taxed at the higher rate unless the company has more than five full-time employees throughout the year or if, in the case of a management services company, it receives its income from a corporation associated with it. In these cases, investment companies and "incorporated employees" will both be eligible for the low tax rate.

*All rates depend on the province in which you reside and whether the provincial corporate rates remain as they are.

Assuming you qualify for the small-business rate, the tax advantages to incorporating are outlined below.

3. MINIMIZING NON-DEDUCTIBLE OR DEPRECIABLE EXPENSES

By doing your own incorporation, you will realize an immediate tax saving in addition to saving on actual costs. As legal fees are not wholly tax deductible as an expense, by doing it yourself you not only save the lawyer's fees, you avoid paying taxes on a non-deductible expense.

4. SPLITTING YOUR INCOME

With a company, you can effectively "split" your income. For example, say your business made $75 000 last year as a proprietorship. This entire amount would be considered your personal income and be taxed at approximately 36%* (assuming you're eligible for the basic personal and CPP non-refundable tax credits).

On the other hand, if you have incorporated, $25 000 could be paid to you personally as salary or bonus and $50 000 could be left in the company. This $50 000 would be taxed at the rate of 19% if your company qualifies for the small-business tax rate.

On the $25 000 paid out to you personally, you would pay tax of about 18% (assuming you're eligible for the basic CPP and non-refundable tax credits). The top personal marginal rate is about 53%.

This is just one example. In fact, you're allowed to work out any combination that keeps your total tax bill to a minimum, including employing members of your family, as long as they're employed in a bona fide capacity and the payment is reasonable.

At present, a qualifying company's tax rate is only 19% on all earnings below $200 000 per year. Therefore, if your company's earnings are $50 000 a year, you'll pay only 19% in taxes each year.

A further split is also possible. After paying this initial corporate tax, you can then choose to either leave the funds in the company or pay out dividends to the shareholders (which might be, for example, you, your spouse and children). However, starting in 2000, this income splitting opportunity will no longer be available for taxable dividends paid to children under the age of 18. These dividends will be taxable at the highest personal marginal tax rates.

Depending on other sources of income and your personal income tax bracket, it may be more advantageous for one or more of your family members to take payments from the company in the form of dividends alone or in a mixture of dividends and salary.

An individual with no other sources of income will be able to receive approximately $24 000 of Canadian dividends without being subject to tax. This is because of the dividend tax credit. However, the company must be carefully structured for this technique to work properly.

Still, dividends aren't deductible and it's important to limit, if at all possible, net corporate business income to $200 000 in order to pay the lowest corporate income tax rate. Payments of bonuses and salary may therefore be preferable to dividends for corporate earnings in excess of $200 000.

One critical point to keep in mind is that dividend income doesn't qualify as "earned income" for purposes of making a deductible contribution to an RRSP. Further, your income might also be subject to minimum tax.

5. ESTATE PLANNING BENEFITS

With a company, you can obtain substantial estate planning advantages. As this is a technical area and beyond the scope of this book, it won't be discussed at any length.

---

*This rate may be greater or less depending on the province in which you reside.

Suffice it to say that the existence of a company enables you to own a widely diversified portfolio of assets (including all kinds of property) under the ownership of a single entity.

This can be a great advantage from both a tax and an administrative point of view, especially if the company is located in a non-inheritance tax jurisdiction such as British Columbia and the assets are located in an inheritance tax jurisdiction, for example, Washington state.

6. SALARY AND BONUS ACCRUALS

Through a company, you can declare yourself a bonus that is deductible from the company's income but need not be declared by you as income until it is actually paid.

However, the Income Tax Act has rules about how long you can delay declaring the payment as income to you. The rules say that the bonus has to be taken within 179 days from the end of your corporation's tax year in which the bonus was declared. For example, if your company's year end was January 31, and you declared yourself a bonus of $10 000 on January 30, 2000, the company would deduct it as a salary expense for the 1999-2000 year only if the bonus was actually paid by July 29, 2000.

The result is that you would pay personal tax on the bonus in April 2001 (less, of course, the tax the company would have to withhold when it paid you the bonus).

You can see that this gives you some flexibility. To be deductible, these bonuses must be reasonable (in relation to services rendered to the company) and represent a legal liability of the company. (Passing a directors' resolution is adequate.) In addition, there are a number of other tax wrinkles and elections relating to the salary/

dividend/bonus route that any competent tax adviser can tell you about.

The important thing to remember is that you must be careful when planning bonuses to look at the overall tax liability of yourself and your company. If your company is already able to take advantage of the low small-business tax rate, there is little sense in declaring a bonus that will be taxed in your hands as personal income at a slightly higher rate.

If you want to reduce your company's earnings so that it can take advantage of the small-business rate, you might want to declare a bonus payable to yourself and wait before paying it to yourself. In this way you can "even out" the earnings and so pay less total tax.

For example, if you can foresee that your company's earnings for the fiscal year will exceed the amount eligible for the small-business tax rate, declare a bonus for yourself. This may reduce the earnings sufficiently to enable the company to be taxed at the lower small-business rate, or mean less money is taxable at a higher rate. Note that if you do decide to declare yourself a bonus, it must be paid to you within 179 days after year end.

Further, by reducing your corporate profits, you reduce the size of the tax installment payments payable by the corporation and, therefore, improve your cash-flow position.

If you declare dividends payable to yourself, there is no time limit on when they can be paid to you. Once the corporation has paid tax on its profits, dividends can be distributed at any time. This might be beneficial from the point of view of liability for personal income tax.

Remember, whichever method you choose to distribute your corporate earnings, it must be designed to meet the monetary needs and tax liability of both you and the company.

7. EXPENSE DEDUCTIONS

Aside from the fact that operating your business through a limited company may allow you to claim more liberal travel and entertainment expenses, there are perfectly legal and sanctioned ways of using a company to increase expense allowances. For example, country club and similar dues paid by your company on your behalf, while not tax deductible by the company, don't have to be included in your personal income, provided you use the clubs for business entertainment. Therefore, because the company is taxed at a lower rate than you personally, it can earn less than you to net the same amount.

However, business meals and entertainment are only deductible to 50% of their cost. The cost of business meals and entertainment covered by this 50% limitation includes gratuities, overcharges, room rentals at a hotel to provide entertainment, and tickets for entertainment events.

Similarly, if you're arranging life insurance policies, the company can pay the premiums (these are non-deductible, but the money earned to pay the premium is taxed at a lower rate) and any proceeds collected by the company are non-taxable.

8. PLANNING FOR RETIREMENT

In the past, the opportunity for small-business owners to provide for their own retirement was exceptional. Unfortunately, that's no longer the case.

If you're an owner or employee of a corporation, you may not be a beneficiary of your corporation's deferred profit-sharing plan (DPSP). If the company does not have a DPSP or a registered pension plan (RPP), or you're not a beneficiary, your maximum contribution to a registered retirement savings plan (RRSP) can be 18% of your earned income, up to specified limits.

Under pension reform, RRSP dollar limits will increase over time for an individual who isn't a member of a DPSP or an RPP. They are as follows:

2000 — $13 500
2001 — $13 500
2002 — $13 500
2003 — $13 500
2004 — $14 500

Retiring allowances given to employees or employee-shareholders can be transferred to an RRSP, but are limited to $3 500 for each year the employee didn't have vested rights under an RPP or DPSP and $2 000 for each year the employee had such vested benefits. For years of service commencing in 1989, the transfer is limited to $2 000 per year of service.

9. LOANS TO EMPLOYEES AND SHAREHOLDERS

Loans made by a corporation to employees that have a below-market rate of interest or are non-interest bearing will create a taxable benefit to the employee. The taxable benefit will be equal to the difference between the interest rate charged to the employee and the "prescribed" loan rate set by the government.

This rate is adjusted quarterly based on the interest rate paid on 90-day treasury bills for the previous quarter. In other words, on a no-interest loan of $10 000, a prescribed rate of 5% for each quarter in 1999 ($500) is added to the employee's income.

However, on loans to buy shares in their employer company, employees can deduct the interest expense against all other employment income or income from property and dividends. Employees can do this if the shares bought are either preferred shares that yield taxable dividends higher than the prescribed interest rate, or common shares. Thus, no net benefit will be included in the employee's income.

Note: If an employee's interest expense exceeds income from property (e.g., interest and dividends) it will effectively reduce any immediate access to the capital gains exemption by the amount of such excess, until the excess is ultimately absorbed by income from property.

Where the loan is made to allow the employee to buy a car to be used on the job, the maximum deduction for interest costs is $250 per month, subject to certain limitations. There are very complex rules pertaining to the deduction of automobile expenses and your professional advisors should be consulted.

To summarize, low-interest or no-interest loans to employees are no longer as beneficial as they once were, unless they're made to allow the employee to buy shares of the employer company. Loans to allow an employee to buy a car can also be beneficial, but not to the same extent.

10. MANUFACTURING AND PROCESSING CREDIT (M & P)

All active small-business income is taxed at the same rate. As indicated above, the rate on the first $200 000 of this income is about 19%.

For income not eligible for the small-business rate, the manufacturing and processing (M & P) credit reduces the rate of tax on manufacturing income not eligible for the small-business rate to about 39%.

The M & P credit was introduced to reward labour-intensive businesses, supposedly as a stimulus to employment. The Income Tax Act specifically disqualifies certain activities. They are farming, fishing,

logging, on-site job construction, most natural resource activities, and any manufacturing endeavour where manufacturing revenues are less than 10% of the gross sales. Businesses that convert, change, add to, or re-assemble the raw material may qualify. For example, newspapers or printing businesses qualify. Restaurants also qualify because they process food.

Your business is eligible for the M & P credit on the first $200 000 of income if:

(a) your business is involved in primarily manufacturing and processing in Canada,

(b) your business didn't carry on active business outside the country in the year, and

(c) your business didn't carry on activities specifically excluded from the definition of manufacturing and processing.

11. ANTI-AVOIDANCE

The general anti-avoidance rule (GAAR) states that any transaction that results in a significant reduction or even deferral of the tax that might have been payable if the transaction hadn't occurred can be completely ignored, unless it can be shown to have had a bona fide non-tax purpose. However, this rule won't be applied to prohibit access to certain specified tax incentives, including the small-business deduction and the manufacturing and processing tax credit. Therefore, a businessperson is free to use a corporate vehicle to take advantage of these special tax incentives.

12. CONCLUSION

The realization that profits mean taxes tends to cause businesspeople to overreact and become more and more committed to minimizing their tax load. This is totally understandable and perfectly acceptable, as long as the methods used are legal.

The best way to achieve the lowest taxes is to maintain proper and accurate records and ensure that you have at your disposal the legal and accounting expertise you need to help you take advantage of all the opportunities available under the current tax laws.

3
PRELIMINARY MATTERS

1. WHERE TO INCORPORATE

A company is incorporated or "born" upon a certificate of incorporation being issued. You have a choice between incorporating federally under the Canada Business Corporations Act or provincially under the Company Act.

The main advantages to incorporating federally are twofold. First, the corporation is empowered to carry on business in all provinces, provided it becomes registered in each province in which it carries on business. Second, it can use the same name in each province even if there is already a company using a similar name.

The disadvantages to incorporating federally are the higher initial cost and the amount of yearly paperwork that must be done to keep up to date on all filings required by the provinces and the federal Director of the Corporations Branch. It will cost you over $500 to incorporate federally, and, if you hire a lawyer, it will cost you more.

For these reasons, it's often easier for most family-owned or small companies to incorporate in one province and then register in successive provinces as they wish to expand. Usually there's no problem becoming registered in a new province.

This book deals with incorporating a family-owned or small company (i.e., a private or non-reporting corporation) in the province of British Columbia.

2. NON-REPORTING vs. REPORTING COMPANIES

In the past, all companies were classified as "private" or "public." Private companies were usually the small, family-owned companies — in essence, incorporated partnerships. Public companies were commonly the larger companies whose shares were traded on stock exchanges.

This terminology is no longer used. A distinction is now made between "reporting" and "non-reporting" companies. Generally, these terms mean the same as the old definitions of public and private companies.

2.1 Reporting companies

Section 1(1) of the provincial Company Act states:

"reporting company" means a corporation incorporated by or under an Act of the Legislature, other than a corporation continued under section 37,

(a) that has any of its securities listed for trading on any stock exchange wherever located,

(b) that is ordered by the registrar to be a reporting company, or,

(c) that

(i) was or was deemed to be a public company immediately before October 1, 1973,

(ii) had obtained an exemption order, under section 38A of the Companies Act, RSBC 1960, c. 67, if the exemption order was in effect immediately before October 1, 1973,

(iii) with respect to any of its securities, files a prospectus with the executive director and obtains a receipt for it, or

(iv) became an amalgamated company after October 1, 1973, if one of the amalgamating companies was, at the time of amalgamation, a reporting company,

unless the registrar orders that it is not a reporting company;

The significance of this section is that there are no longer any hard and fast rules defining what a public company is and is not. Both the Registrar of Companies and the Executive Director of the Securities Commission have the freedom to consider you a reporting (public) company no matter how many shareholders you have. It all depends on the conduct of the company.

All companies must have directors, officers, and shareholders. But with reporting companies, these positions are occupied by different persons.

The directors of the board of a reporting company usually consist of a group of respected businesspeople who bring to the board a wide variety of business experience. Their function is to act as "watchdogs" over the officers and to protect the interests of the shareholders who elect them on an annual basis. Unfortunately, for a variety of reasons, this objective is not always attained.

Most officers of large reporting companies are hired professionals who are in charge of the day-to-day activities. In many companies, they also wield the greatest influence on the overall operations of the company. Usually the two or three top officers of the company are also members of the board of directors, but not necessarily. For example, a vice-president in a reporting company may not sit on the board of directors, and will almost certainly not own enough shares of the company to affect corporate policy from a shareholder's position. His or her effect on the operations of the company depends solely on his or her position as an officer of the company.

The last group in a reporting company, but certainly the largest in terms of numbers, consists of shareholders. In reporting companies, shareholders are the theoretical "owners" of the company, which, in turn, owns the assets. Shares represent ownership. However, ownership of shares doesn't usually give the shareholder the right or power to run the company. (**Note:** The term "shareholder" is interchangeable with the term "member," and both mean the same thing. In the Company Act, shareholders are always referred to as members.)

In theory, the final authority for a company's operations rests with the shareholders. In reality, this is often untrue. Shareholders of a reporting company are often spread all over the country, so very few attend the annual meeting. Most shareholders want only a return on their investment (dividends) and an increase in the value of their shares; they don't want to run a company. If the company doesn't perform satisfactorily, the shareholders rarely call the management or directors to task or replace them. They simply sell their shares.

Furthermore, many shareholders lack the competence and experience to run the business properly, so they hesitate to question the activities of managing officers or directors. Also, the usual wide dispersal of shareholders means that it would take a great deal of time, money, and effort for a group of reform-minded individuals to obtain enough support to seriously challenge the management or directors of the company.

The structure of a reporting company can be illustrated by this diagram:

XYZ LTD.

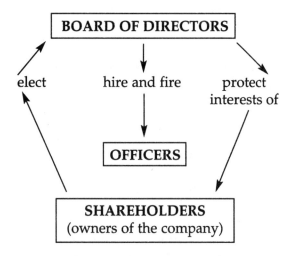

2.2 Non-reporting companies

Obviously, not all businesses incorporate with the intention of selling shares to the public to raise large amounts of capital. To give small businesses the advantages of incorporation, a different type of company, the non-reporting company, was created by the provincial Company Act.

The essential characteristics of a non-reporting company in British Columbia are as follows:

(a) There is some restriction on the transfer of shares.

(b) You cannot offer shares or debentures of the company for sale to the public.

(c) The directors, officers, and shareholders are often the same people.

(d) Only one director is required (a reporting company must have three).

A policy statement issued by the Securities Commission provides some guidelines as to what a non-reporting company is:

(a) The stock is held by relatively few holders.

(b) The management and ownership are substantially identical or there exists a community of relationship between the members, i.e., based on family, business, social, or other common interest.

(c) The stock is not traded in any securities market.

(d) The company has never made an offering of its securities to the public.

(e) The stock is subject to restrictions on transfer.

The policy statement goes on to say that "even though all of the ingredients of a close corporation may exist" in the applicant company, the "overriding consideration will be the security holders' and public's need and right to know what is transpiring" in the company.

The first four points in the policy statement are self-explanatory. The last point recognizes that small companies operate like partnerships and, as such, need control over who becomes a "partner," that is, a shareholder. Therefore, some sort of restriction on the transfer of shares is needed in the case of a small company.

This share restriction transfer is contained in the company's "articles" — a document setting out the rules for the conduct of the company (see chapter 4). If you look in the model set of articles in Sample 8, you'll see the share transfer restriction in part 24. This clause combines the need for control over transferability with the protection needed by a shareholder who wishes to sell out and receive a fair market price for his or her shares.

As you can see, a share transfer restriction is really a double-edged sword. If some other shareholder were attempting to sell his or her shares, you would like to see severe restriction on transferability to avoid the intrusion of an unwanted "partner" shareholder. However, if it were you who wanted to sell, the fewer restrictions on transferability the better, because you could approach many more buyers.

The structure of a non-reporting corporation is essentially like an "incorporated partnership" because it usually consists of one, two, or three people who are close friends, business associates, or family members.

Each individual may hold two or three positions in the company. It's not unusual for one person to be, at the same time, a shareholder, officer, and director. For example, if you have a family company in which the husband has 50% of the shares, the wife 25%, and a son the other 25%, it is likely that these persons will be the only directors. They will then also act as the officers. Quite often, both the husband and wife will be the sole directors as well as shareholders. In this case, usually both are directors, officers, and shareholders. Be careful, however, not to confuse the duties and responsibilities of shareholder, officer, and director, even when the persons occupying these positions are the same.

The annual general meeting of a non-reporting company is one of many instances when you will wear more than one hat at the same time (see chapter 11 for a discussion of annual general meetings). For example, in the daily activities of your business, you function as an officer. If you decide, however, to branch out into a new area, or to purchase or sell company assets, you are wearing the hat of a director, as all officers must refer important matters to the board of directors. When you attend the annual meeting and vote on the issue, purchase, or sale of shares or of substantially all of the assets of the company, you function as a shareholder. Shareholders always have the last say on any issue seriously affecting the nature of the company because the shareholders are the owners of the company.

In many companies, the partners in business are not 50-50 owners when it comes to ownership of shares. This puts the minority shareholder (who holds less than 50% of the shares) in a precarious position with regard to the majority shareholder (who holds more than 50% of the shares). Ideally, if you're involved in a two-person corporation where the parties aren't family relations, the shareholdings should be equal. If this cannot be done, the minority shareholder should obtain competent legal advice to protect his or her interest. Further, if one partner is transferring substantial assets to the company, professional advice should be obtained.

You might ask what happens if the shares are divided equally and the "partner" shareholders disagree over a basic issue and a deadlock results. The answer is that either the assets are sold and the business is wound up, or one party buys out the other. (See chapter 10 for more information on this.) This reflects the basic nature of a non-reporting company as being like an "incorporated partnership." When partners in a business have irreconcilable differences, the partnership must be dissolved. The same is true in a small company. But an equal split of the shares encourages co-operation. When this balance is altered it will, of necessity, affect the relationship of the shareholders in the company.

To avoid this problem, some companies provide for what is called a "casting vote" provision in their articles, which gives the chairperson of the meeting or the president a second casting vote in a deadlock. Frequently, however, a casting vote provision merely aggravates the dispute rather than resolves it.

3. ONE-PERSON COMPANIES

In British Columbia, the Company Act allows the formation of one-person companies.

This means that the same person may be the president, secretary, sole director, *and* sole shareholder, as long as that person resides in British Columbia.

The evolution of one-person companies recognizes that many people are in business solely with and for themselves (the so-called incorporated proprietorship). Rather than have a "nominal" second shareholder who performs no real function and serves no purpose, it was considered desirable to allow a single person to gain the advantages of incorporation.

The procedures for incorporation are the same for the one-person company as for any other company.

4. NPL (SPECIALLY LIMITED) COMPANIES

The British Columbia Company Act also provides for a special category of companies called the "specially limited company" or "non-personal liability" (NPL) company. The term non-personal liability is a bit misleading in the sense that all companies, not just NPL companies, provide limited liability for their shareholders. But NPL companies are different from other companies in the following ways:

(a) NPL companies are restricted to high-risk ventures such as exploring for, developing, mining, or producing minerals, coal, or petroleum and natural gas.

(b) (Par value) shares of NPL companies can be sold at a greater discount than (par value) shares in a regular non-reporting company (where the discount is limited to 25%).

NPL companies can sell shares at any discount because the mining, oil, and gas industries are very risky and require a great deal of capital. Consequently, the promoters are allowed to raise capital by selling the shares at greatly varying prices.

Unfortunately, promoters can and do abuse this privilege. One of the more common gimmicks they use is to offer shares at so-called discounts from par value, representing these shares as being offered at special discount prices. This is misleading, as the term "par value" is even more meaningless in an NPL company than in an ordinary limited company. (See chapter 7 for a discussion of par value and without par value shares.) Be wary of "friends" who offer you shares in an NPL company at a special discount. Chances are nil that you'll actually be getting a deal.

You should also understand that without par value shares cannot be sold at what most consumers would call a genuine discount, because the term "without par value" means that the shares have no stated value. They are worth only whatever people will pay for them in the marketplace. Because discounts are meaningless for without par value shares, most mining and oil companies simply use par value shares and discount them as much as they wish.

As mentioned earlier, the prime objective of most new NPL mining companies is to raise enough capital to carry on some type of exploration program. This is done by "floating" or issuing stock. A popular method of raising capital is to sell "cheap" stock (i.e., heavily discounted) in large blocks to investors who will, in turn, resell at higher prices. This produces a "pyramid" effect in the distribution chain. Directors often provide liberal payment terms to induce investors to buy and sell stock.

For example, there's normally a 14-day grace period between the ordering of the stock and payment for it, and the directors often extend this to 60 days so the investors can resell the stock and, in effect, avoid having to pay for it themselves.

The regulations governing incorporation of a specially limited or NPL company are virtually the same as for a regular company with the following exceptions:

(a) The objects of an NPL company must be restricted to those found in clause 2 of Form 2 in the second schedule of the Company Act (the sample memorandum found in Sample 7). This clause essentially states that the company is restricted to doing business in the exploration, development, mining, or production of minerals, coal, or petroleum and natural gas.

(b) The name of an NPL company must include the words "non-personal liability" or the abbreviation "NPL."

(c) An NPL company is restricted in its financial dealings. It cannot lend money or guarantee the debts of any person or corporation, nor can it finance or help finance any other person or business venture.

(d) The letters "NPL" must be displayed whenever the company name is used or displayed, that is, in all advertisements, name plates, or correspondence.

Because of these restrictions, most corporate lawyers today don't recommend this type of company be used at all, even for mining or oil and gas companies. In most cases, you'd be just as well off with a regular non-reporting company because it —

(a) avoids restrictions on financial dealings,

(b) can issue (par value) shares at a discount of up to 25%, and

(c) can issue without par value shares at whatever price it chooses.

4
INCORPORATION PROCEDURE FOR A NON-REPORTING COMPANY

The following is a general, abbreviated, step-by-step list of the procedures necessary to incorporate a non-reporting company in British Columbia, together with a brief explanation of each step. (For a checklist of these procedures, see the Appendix.)

During and after your incorporation, you'll be dealing with the Registrar of Companies. For inquiries in person or delivered by courier, the address is:

Registrar of Companies
Ministry of Finance &
Corporate Relations
2nd Floor, 940 Blanshard Street
Victoria, BC V8W 3E6

For all inquiries by mail, the address is:

Registrar of Companies
Ministry of Finance &
Corporate Relations

PO Box 9431 Stn. Prov. Govt.
Victoria, BC V8W 9V3

The telephone number is:

(250) 387-7848 or (604) 775-1041
in Greater Vancouver

The Registrar's office is open from 8:30 a.m. to 4:30 p.m., Monday through Friday.

The Registrar's fees are found in the Third Schedule of the Company Act, which are reprinted in Table 1 for your convenience.

Note: All documents submitted to the companies office must have the postal codes on all addresses.

1.   GET A COPY OF THE ACT

Anyone proposing to incorporate a company should obtain a copy of the provincial

TABLE 1
INCORPORATION FEES*

Effective October 18, 1999:	
For incorporation (basic fee)	$300
To approve or reserve a name	30
Certification of Memorandum and articles	25
For registration of an extra-provincial company (basic fee)	300
For changing the name of a British Columbia company (basic fee)	100
For changing the name of an extra-provincial company (basic fee)	100
For restoration of a company or an extra-provincial company (basic fee)	300
For a certified copy of any document	25
For filing an annual report	35
Priority service	100

*Note that while these fees are current at the time of publication, all fees are subject to change without notice. For current fees, telephone the Registrar of Companies before submitting your documents.

Company Act. You may buy it from the publisher (see order form at the front of this book) or order the act from Crown Publications in Victoria; call (250) 386-4636. In Vancouver, you may also buy the Company Act from International Travel Maps and Books; call (604) 687-3320.

2. CHOOSE A NAME

A company, like a person, must have a name, but unfortunately it's not as easy to pick a name for a company as for a baby. When you select a name for your company, you must choose a name that is acceptable not only to you but also the Registrar of Companies.

In broad terms, the Registrar will usually approve a company name so long as it isn't identical to and doesn't closely resemble any existing company names. Names that are similar to existing company names will be rejected because they may cause confusion.

One of the easiest ways to check out existing names is to look in the telephone directory for the names of companies already doing business in your area. Trade and corporation directories, available in any large library, will help you find other protected names of Canadian organizations.

In addition, your name must also have the following three components:

(a)   A distinctive element

(b)   A descriptive element

(c)   A corporate designation

What you want to achieve is a name that is both distinctive and accurately describes the type of business you intend to carry on.

2.1   Distinctive element

The first part of your name must start with a distinctive word or phrase such as your name, a geographical location, a made-up word, a coined phrase, or initials. For example, you might choose "Quiggly" as in "Quiggly Cleaners Ltd." for a drycleaning company. "Quiggly" is quite distinctive.

Beware, however, of words like "Western," which is one of those words that has been used in names so frequently that it's no longer distinctive. Other words that suffer the same fate are "Northern," "Pacific," "Universal," and "Maple Leaf."

You can also use numerals as the distinctive element in your company name, for example, "2468 Cleaning Ltd." It would be better, though, to use "Quiggly" or some other phrase that is more distinctive than "2468."

2.2   Descriptive element

The second part of your company name must describe the type of business the company will be operating. For example, "Cleaners" in "Quiggly Cleaners Ltd." gives potential customers a good idea of what the company's business will be.

2.3   Corporate designation

The third and last part of your name must be the corporate designation, for example, "Limited," "Ltd.," "Corporation," "Corp.," "Incorporated," or "Inc."

A year can be part of your company name, as long as it's the year of incorporation, amalgamation, or registration, for example, "Fraser Valley Machinery (2000) Ltd."

Of course, in the case of an NPL company you'll also have to include the words "non-personal liability" or the abbreviation NPL. This is usually in brackets at the end of the name, for example, "Drydock Mines Ltd. (NPL)."

2.4   Names to avoid

Many names are routinely rejected by the Registrar of Companies. You'll want to avoid these.

When selecting your name, stay away from using the words "Institute," "Condominium," or "Co-operative," which are restricted to specific organizations in many provinces.

Names that imply a connection with or approval of the Royal Family are also routinely rejected. Further, names that imply government approval or the sponsorship of a branch, service, or department are frequently not acceptable. That eliminates words such as "Parliament Hill," "RCMP," or "Legislative" from the list of choices.

The Registrar will probably not approve a name that could be construed as obscene or that is too general in that it only describes the quality, goods, or function of the services. Companies with names like "General Motors" and "Best Foods" have more or less taken up these choices.

Last, but not least, stay well away from the names of companies already in existence (or the common contractions of their names). For example, a name like "Xerox Construction Ltd." implies that your resources are connected with those of Xerox. This is only acceptable if true. If it's not true, Xerox may accuse you of trying to "steal" the name and may bring a "passing off" suit against you.

2.5 Successful names

Generally, you should remember that the most successful proposals are likely to be among the following:

(a) A coined word (perhaps a combination of incorporators' names) plus a descriptive word (e.g., Kenbar Dolls Ltd.).

(b) The full name of an individual (e.g., John Albert Doe Ltd.). However, be careful about using your name as the company name. First, depending on the business you are in, you may get people calling

you at home at all hours. Second, if your company goes bankrupt, your reputation may be ruined for many years simply because of the name. And third, if you ever sell out, your name will go with the business and somebody else might run it into the ground, with the same result as if you had gone bankrupt.

(c) The name of an individual combined with a descriptive word (e.g., Doe Explorations Ltd. or Jane's Shoe Store Inc.).

(d) The combination of a distinctive geographic name plus a descriptive word (e.g., Fraser Valley Machinery Inc.), provided the company is connected with or operating in that area.

2.6 Numbered companies

If you just want to use the incorporation number for your company name, the Registrar of Companies will select one for you. The number given will depend on the next available number at the time of incorporation. Your numbered company will read like "654321 BC Ltd." or "654321 British Columbia Inc."

You can indicate you just want a numbered company by leaving a seven-letter space (about half an inch) in front of the words "BC Ltd." or "British Columbia Ltd." on your memorandum and other documents wherever you need to give the name of your company (e.g., _____ BC Ltd.).

Note: You don't need to reserve your name or pay a name reservation fee if you use this procedure.

3. HAVE THE NAME RESERVED

To have your chosen name searched and reserved, submit a list of no more than three names, in order of preference, to the

Registrar of Companies for approval, along with the $30 fee (cheque or money order payable to the Minister of Finance and Corporate Relations). You can also submit your request at an OSBR computer workstation (see chapter 1) or nearest government agent office.

You do this by letter or by filling out a Name Approval Request Form (see Sample 5). For a copy of the form, call (250) 356-2893 or, in Greater Vancouver, (604) 775-1044, or download the form onto your computer from the Ministry of Finance and Corporate Relations' Web site at <www.fin.gov. bc.ca/registries/corppg>. You can also obtain the form at an OSBR computer workstation or nearest government agent office.

(If you have a BC Online account, you may reserve by fax. However, there's no reason to open an account unless you plan to do a number of separate name reservations. If you do wish to open an account, call BC Online at 1-800-663-6102.)

It normally takes the Registrar's office two to three working days to process your request. You'll be informed of the results in the same way you submitted your request. If you mailed your request, you will be notified by mail; if you went in person to a government agent office, that office will contact you.

Once the Registrar has approved a name, the approved name will be reserved for 56 days, and you'll be given a reservation number which should be quoted in your filing letter when you send in your incorporation documents. You therefore have 56 days from the date of approval of the name to complete your incorporation. If it's not completed within that time, someone else may claim the name and you would then have to start all over again. In the event of an unforeseen delay in proceeding with incorporation, the Registrar will, for an additional fee, reserve the approved name for a further 56 days upon receipt of a request in writing.

For a numbered company, the Registrar will assign a number at the time of incorporation. You don't need to reserve your name or pay the name reservation fee (see section **2.1** above).

4.   PREPARE THE MEMORANDUM

The memorandum is your company's "constitution." The memorandum must be in the prescribed form shown at the back of the Company Act, and it must be printed or typewritten (use white letter-size paper). Blank forms are enclosed in the *Incorporation Forms and Disk for BC* kit, available from the publisher of this book. You can order this kit (see the order form at the front of this book) or buy it at any stationery store. You'll need to prepare two copies to submit to the Registrar of Companies (two sets are enclosed in the self-incorporation kit).

The memorandum must show the name of the company, the authorized capital, and the number of each class of share taken by the first shareholders (subscribers). You can see a completed memorandum in Sample 6. A memorandum for a non-personal liability company follows in Sample 7.

Under the Company Act, a British Columbia company has all the powers and capacities of a natural person. This means your company may engage in any sort of business that it chooses (restrictions do exist for those who wish to form trust companies, insurance companies, railway lines, and clubs).

If you wish, you may impose restrictions on your company if, for example, you wish to protect your investment funds by insisting that the company invest in mortgages only. These cases are rare, however.

You may use par value shares, or shares without par value, or both. (For more information on shares and par value, see chapter 7.) Sample 6 and Sample 7 use shares without par value because they

SAMPLE 5
NAME APPROVAL FORM

BRITISH COLUMBIA

Ministry of Finance
and Corporate Relations
Corporate and Personal
Property Registries

Mailing Address:
PO Box 9431 Stn Prov Govt
Victoria BC V8W 9V3
Location:
2nd Floor – 940 Blanshard Street
Victoria BC

NAME APPROVAL REQUEST
(WEBFORM)

DOCUMENT
CONTROL NUMBER **NR**

Please quote this number on all correspondence

Fax: (250) 356-1428

Phone: (250) 356-2893 or
775-1044 (Greater Vancouver only)

Freedom of Information and Protection of Privacy Act (FIPPA)
The personal information requested on this form is made
available to the public under the authority of the *Company Act.*
Questions about how the *FIPPA* applies to this personal
information can be directed to the Administrative Analyst,
Corporate and Personal Property Registries at (250) 356-0944,
PO Box 9431 Stn Prov Govt, Victoria BC V8W 9V3.

INSTRUCTIONS:

• Please retain the yellow copy for your records. The Name
Reservation Office will notify you by letter once your request
is completed.

• **Please type or print clearly.**

• *SHADED AREAS ARE FOR OFFICE USE ONLY.*

PRIORITY REQUEST – *Additional fee required*

☐ **YES** – This is a priority request and I have
enclosed an additional fee for this service.

ROUTING SLIP NO.	DEBIT BCOL ACCOUNT NO.
FOLIO NO.	DEPOSIT ACCOUNT TRANSACTION NO.
GOVT. AGENT TRANSACTION DATE YYYY MM DD	DATE RECEIVED YYYY MM DD
GOVT. AGENT TRANSACTION NO.	GOVT. AGENT AMOUNT COLLECTED $

APPLICANT SURNAME	FIRST NAME AND INITIALS
Doe	Jean J.

ADDRESS 321 Yin Street

CITY Vancouver	PROVINCE BC	POSTAL CODE Z 1 P 1 G 0

APPLICANT PHONE NO. 604-876-1234	APPLICANT FAX NO. 604-876-1235	CONTACT PERSON NAME Jean J. Doe

Indicate what the name request is for: (In order for this request to be completed, one box must be (✔) ticked)

☒ CORPORATION   ☐ PROPRIETORSHIP/PARTNERSHIP   ☐ SOCIETY   ☐ FINANCIAL INSTITUTION   ☐ COOPERATIVE ASSOCIATION

Is this request for an extra provincial registration in B.C.? ☐ YES ☒ NO	IF YES, SUPPLY THE JURISDICTION	NATURE OF BUSINESS Grocery Retail Business

ADDITIONAL INFORMATION

Name Request *(first choice)* **PLEASE TYPE OR PRINT CLEARLY**

STAR GROCERIES LTD.

Name Request *(second choice)* **PLEASE TYPE OR PRINT CLEARLY**

MOON GROCERIES LTD.

Name Request *(third choice)* **PLEASE TYPE OR PRINT CLEARLY**

APOLLO GROCERIES LTD.

FIN 708B Rev. 1999 / 5 / 6   FORWARD ORIGINAL TO NAME RESERVATION OFFICE   RETAIN A COPY FOR YOUR RECORDS

SAMPLE 6
MEMORANDUM

Form 1
(Section 5)

COMPANY ACT

MEMORANDUM

_____We_____ wish to be formed into a company with limited liability under the Company Act in pursuance of this Memorandum.

1. The name of the company is

    J & J Industries Ltd.

2. The authorized capital of the company consists of

    Ten thousand (10 000) Common shares without par value

3. _____We_____ agree to take the number and kind of shares in the company set opposite_____our_____ name.

Full Name(s), Resident Address(es)
and Occupation(s) of Subscriber(s)

Number and Kind of Shares
taken by Subscriber(s)

John Doe

John Doe
Teacher
111 A Street
Anywhere, BC
Z1P 0G0

Fifty Common shares
without par value

Jack Doe

Jack Doe
Computer consultant*
222 B Street
Anywhere, BC
Z1P 0G0

Fifty Common shares
without par value

Total Shares Taken:

One hundred Common shares
Without par value

Dated the __15th__ day of_____May_____, 200 _-___.

*If you are self-employed, you must specify the nature of your work.

SAMPLE 7
MEMORANDUM FOR AN NPL COMPANY

Form 1
(Section 5)

COMPANY ACT

MEMORANDUM

I/We wish to be formed into a specially limited company under the Company Act in pursuance of this Memorandum.

See section 16 (Company Act). It requires these words or their initials after the name. Paragraph 2 may not be added to, but deletions are permitted.

1. The name of the company is J & J EXPLORATIONS LTD. (Non-Personal Liability).

2. The business that the company is permitted to carry on are restricted to the following:
   (a) exploring for, developing, mining, smelting, milling, and refining materials and coal;
   (b) exploring for, developing, and producing petroleum and natural gas.

Paragraph 3 may be added to, but deletions are not permitted.

3. The company is restricted from exercising the following powers:
   (a) to lend money or to guarantee the contract of any person or corporation, wheresoever incorporated;
   (b) to raise or assist in raising money for, or to aid by way of bonus, promise, endorsement, guarantee of debentures or other securities or otherwise, any person or corporation, wheresoever incorporated.

If you have both par and no par value shares, refer to section 19(3) for description, otherwise omit the reference to the kind of shares you do not have.

4. The authorized capital of the company consists of____3 000 000 to 5 000 000____ shared divided into_____ shares with a par value of _____ each and_____ shares without par value.

Any additional provisions here.

5. I/We agree to take the number (and kind) (and class) of shares in the company set opposite my/our name(s).

FULL NAMES, RESIDENT ADDRESSES, CITIZENSHIP, AND OCCUPATION OF SUBSCRIBERS	NUMBER (AND KIND) (AND CLASS) OF SHARES TAKEN BY SUBSCRIBERS
John Doe John Doe, teacher 111A Street Anywhere, BC Z1P 0G0 Prospector (Canadian)	Fifty (50) common shares without par value
Jack Doe Jack Doe, Businessman 222B Street Anywhere, BC Z1P 0G0 Prospector (Canadian)	Fifty (50) common shares without par value

Total shares taken: One Hundred (100) common shares without par value.

DATED the___15th___ day of_____May_____ 200 -____

Note: The provisions of the memorandum may be altered only to the extent and in the manner provided by part 8 of the Company Act.

30

more accurately reflect the true share value than par value shares.

If you want a more complicated share structure, the rights and restrictions have to be detailed in the memorandum or articles. It's more common to see them in the articles. If the rights and restrictions are contained in the articles, the description of the classes of shares in the capital clause of the memorandum should state, for example, "The class B shares and the preference shares shall have special rights and restrictions set forth in the articles of the company." If they're detailed in the memorandum, the articles must explain this (see paragraph 2.1 in Sample 8).

Where there are classes of common shares and the only difference between them is the right to vote, then this difference should be part of the designation of the classes in the capital clause.

The sample memorandum for the NPL company (Sample 7) reflects the fact that most companies of this sort would issue three to five million shares, while ten thousand shares would be adequate for most normal non-reporting companies (see Sample 6). Both types of companies may increase the number of shares at a later date at no extra cost if they wish to.

Both copies of the memorandum must be signed by each subscriber (person who originally forms the company). The two subscribers in Sample 6 and Sample 7 have signed the memorandum and have written the number of shares each is subscribing for next to their names.

By signing the memorandum as a subscriber, you are assuming the duties and responsibilities of a director until the first meeting of the shareholders, when new directors are elected and a notice of change of directors is filed. (See chapter 13 for a discussion on directors' duties.)

Remember, the minimum number of shares you can subscribe for is one. It's recommended that the subscribers be the intended shareholders. However, someone like a lawyer can incorporate the company by taking only one or two shares and then transferring them to the intended shareholders at the first meeting of directors. (See chapter 12 for information on directors' meetings.)

5. PREPARE THE ARTICLES

Your articles are the rules and regulations that govern the conduct of the company and its shareholders, directors, and officers. You will need to prepare two copies of the articles. The articles in Sample 8 are adapted for a simple non-reporting company and are available in the *Incorporation Forms and Disk for BC* kit. You can buy this kit from the publisher (see the order form at the front of this book) or at most stationery stores. Examine the set of articles in Sample 8, even if you wish to use another set. **Note:** You must sign both sets of articles.

The Company Act includes a different set of articles in its Table A. Do not adopt these articles set out in the Company Act, Table A, unless you've consulted one of the Incorporation Examiners at the Registrar of Companies in Victoria. If you decide to adopt the Table A articles, state this on a separate sheet and include your company name and your name and address. This sheet must be signed and dated by you.

Note: The sample articles in Sample 8 are different from the Table A articles included at the back of the Company Act. You don't need to consult an incorporation examiner if you are using the Sample 8 articles shown in this book, also contained in the *Incorporation Forms and Disk for BC* kit.

Every non-reporting company must include and comply with provisions in its articles that restrict the transfer of shares and

SAMPLE 8
ARTICLES OF INCORPORATION

ARTICLES
TABLE OF CONTENTS

SAMPLE 8 — Continued

SAMPLE 8 — Continued

"COMPANY ACT"
ARTICLES OF

J & J Industries

PART 1 — INTERPRETATION

1.1

In these Articles, unless the context otherwise requires:

(a) "Board of Directors" or "Board" means the directors of the Company for the time being;

(b) "casual vacancy" shall mean any vacancy occurring in the Board of Directors of the Company save and except for a vacancy occurring at an annual general meeting of the Company;

(c) "Company Act" means the Company Act of the Province of British Columbia from time to time in force and all amendments thereto and includes all regulations and amendments thereto made pursuant to that Act;

(d) "directors" means the directors of the Company for the time being;

(e) "month" means calendar month;

(f) "ordinary resolution" has the meaning assigned thereto by the Company Act;

(g) "register" means the register of members to be kept pursuant to the Company Act;

(h) "registered address" of a member shall be his address as recorded in the register;

(i) "registered address" of a director means his address as recorded in the Company's register of directors to be kept pursuant to the Company Act;

(j) "reporting company" has the meaning assigned thereto by the Company Act;

(k) "seal" means the common seal of the Company, if the Company has one;

(l) "special resolution" has the meaning assigned thereto by the Company Act.

1.2

Expressions referring to writing shall be construed as including references to printing, lithography, typewriting, photography and other modes of representing or reproducing words in a visible form.

1.3

Words importing the singular include the plural and vice versa; and words importing a male person include a female person and a corporation.

1.4

The definitions in the Company Act shall, with the necessary changes and so far as applicable, apply to these Articles.

1.5

The regulations contained in Table A in the First Schedule to the Company Act shall not apply to the Company.

PART 2 — SHARES AND SHARE CERTIFICATES

2.1

The authorized capital of the Company shall consist of shares of a class or classes, which may be divided into one or more series, as described in the Memorandum of the Company and shall be evidenced or represented in the form of a certificate, and each class of shares shall have a distinct form of certificate.

2.2

Every share certificate issued by the Company shall be in such form as the directors approve and shall comply with the Company Act.

2.3

Every member is entitled, without charge, to one certificate representing the share or shares of each class held by him or upon paying a sum not exceeding the amount permitted by the Company Act, as the directors may from time to time determine, several certificates each for one or more of those shares; provided that, in respect of a share or shares held jointly by several persons, the Company shall not be bound to issue more than one certificate, and delivery of a certificate for a share to one of several joint holders or to his duly authorized agent shall be sufficient delivery to all; and provided further that the Company shall not be bound to issue certificates representing redeemable shares, if such shares are to be redeemed within one month of the date on which they were allotted. Any share certificate may be sent through the post by registered pre-paid mail to the member entitled thereto at his registered address, and the Company shall not be liable for any loss occasioned to the member owing to any such share certificate so sent being lost in the post or stolen.

2.4

Certificates shall be available for delivery by the Company within one month after the allotment of and payment in full for any of its shares, or within one month after the delivery to the Company of an instrument of transfer, unless the conditions of the share otherwise provide, or where the Company has issued shares with a special right to convert attached thereto, within one month after receipt by the Company of the share certificate for the share to be converted properly tendered for conversion.

2.5

If a share certificate:

(a) is worn out or defaced, the directors may, upon production to them of that certificate and upon such other terms if any, as they may think fit, order the certificate to be cancelled and may issue a new certificate in lieu thereof;

(b) is lost, stolen or destroyed, then upon proof thereof to the satisfaction of the directors and upon such indemnity, if any, as the directors deem adequate being given, a new share certificate in place thereof shall be issued to the person entitled to the lost, stolen or destroyed certificate, or

(c) represents more than one share and the registered owner thereof surrenders it to the Company with a written request that the Company issue registered in his name two or more certificates each representing a specified number of shares and in the aggregate representing the same number of shares as the certificate so surrendered, the Company shall cancel the certificate so surrendered and issue in place thereof certificates in accordance with the request.

A sum, not exceeding that permitted by the Company Act, as the directors may from time to time fix, shall be paid to the Company for each certificate issued under this Article.

2.6

Except as required by law or statute or these Articles, no person shall be recognized by the Company as holding any share upon any trust, and the Company shall not be bound by or compelled in any way to recognize (even when having notice thereof) any equitable, contingent, future or partial interest in any share or any interest in any fractional part of a share or (except only as by law or statute or these Articles provided or as ordered by a court of competent jurisdiction) any other rights in respect of any share except an absolute right to the entirety thereof in the registered holder.

2.7

Every share certificate shall be signed manually by at least one officer or director of the Company, or by or on behalf of a registrar, branch registrar, transfer agent or branch transfer agent of the Company and any additional signatures may be printed or otherwise mechanically reproduced and a certificate signed in either of those fashions shall be as valid as if signed manually, notwithstanding that any person whose signature is so printed or mechanically reproduced on a share certificate has ceased to hold the office that he is stated on such certificate to hold at the date of the issue of a share certificate.

2.8

The certificates of shares registered in the name of two or more persons shall be delivered to the person first named on the register.

PART 3 — ISSUE OF SHARES

3.1

The Company may commence business forthwith upon its incorporation notwithstanding that any part of the capital of the Company may remain unallotted or unsubscribed.

3.2

Subject to the Company Act and any provision contained in a resolution passed at a general meeting authorizing any alteration of the capital of the Company, the unissued shares of the Company together with any shares of the Company purchased or redeemed by the Company and not cancelled shall be under the control of the directors who may, subject to the rights of the holders of the shares of the Company for the time being, issue, allot, sell, grant options on, or otherwise dispose of such shares to such persons, including directors, and upon such terms and conditions, and at such price or for such consideration, as the directors, in their absolute discretion, may determine.

3.3

While the Company is not a reporting company and if the directors are so required by the Company Act, they shall, before allotting any shares of the Company, first offer such shares pro rata to the members in the following manner:

    (a)   if the shares are not divided into classes the directors shall make such offer pro rata to the members;

    (b)   if there are classes of shares, the directors shall make such offer pro rata to the members holding all shares of the class proposed to be allotted and if any shares remain, the directors shall then offer the remaining shares pro rata to the other members;

    (c)   any such offer shall be made by notice specifying the number of shares offered and limiting a time for acceptance which shall not be less than seven days;

    (d), after the expiration of the time for acceptance or on receipt of written confirmation from the person to whom the offer is made that he declines to accept the offer, and if there are no other members holding shares who should first receive an offer, the directors may for three months thereafter offer the shares to such persons and in such manner as they think most beneficial to the Company; but the offer to those persons shall not be at a price less than, or on terms more favorable than, the offer to the members; and

    (e)   the directors shall not be required to make such an offer to a member who has waived in writing his right to receive such offer and, while the Company is a reporting company, such pro rata offering need not be made.

3.4

The Company may at any time, subject to the Company Act, pay a commission or allow a discount to any person in consideration of his subscribing or agreeing to subscribe, or procuring or agreeing to procure subscriptions, whether absolutely or conditionally, for any shares of the Company, which commission or discount, except where the Company is a specially limited company, shall not, in the aggregate exceed twenty-five percent (25%) of the subscription price. Where the Company is a specially limited company, such discount or commission shall not exceed ninety-five percent (95%) of the subscription price or the par value, whichever is the greater. The company may also pay such brokerage as may be lawful.

3.5

The Company may pay such brokerage fee or other consideration as may be lawful for or in connection with the sale or placement of its securities.

3.6

Except as provided for by the Company Act, no share may be issued until it is fully paid by the receipt by the Company of the full consideration therefor in cash, property or past services actually performed for the Company. The document evidencing indebtedness of the person to whom the shares are allotted is not property for the purpose of this Article. The value of property and services for the purpose of this Article shall be the fair market value thereof as determined by the directors by resolution.

3.7

The directors may determine the price or consideration at or for which shares without par value may be issued.

3.8

The Company may, subject to the Company Act, issue share purchase warrants upon such terms and conditions as the directors shall determine, which share purchase warrants may be issued alone or in conjunction with debentures, debenture stock, bonds, shares or any other security issued or created by the Company from time to time.

PART 4 — SHARE TRANSFERS

4.1

Subject to the restrictions, if any, set forth in these Articles, (see Part 24), any member may transfer his shares by instrument in writing executed by or on behalf of such member and delivered to the Company or its transfer agent. The instrument of transfer of any share of the Company shall be in the form, if any, on the back of the Company's form of share certificates, and in any form which the directors may approve. If the directors so require, each instrument of transfer shall be in respect of only one class of share.

4.2

Every instrument of transfer shall be executed by the transferor and left at the registered office of the Company or at the office of its transfer agent or registrar for registration together with the share certificate for the shares to be transferred and such other evidence, if any, as the directors or the transfer agent or registrar may require to prove the title of the transferor or his right to transfer the shares. All instruments of transfer where the transfer is registered shall be retained by the Company or its transfer agent or registrar and any instrument of transfer, where the transfer is not registered, shall be returned to the person depositing the same together with the share certificate which accompanied the same when tendered for registration. The transferor shall remain the holder of the share until the name of the transferee is entered on the register in respect of that share.

4.3

The signature of the registered owner of any shares, or of his duly authorized attorney, upon the instrument of transfer constitutes an authority to the Company to register the shares specified in the instrument of transfer in the name of the person named in that instrument of transfer as transferee or, if no person is so named, then in any name designated in writing by the person depositing the share certificate and the instrument of transfer with the Company or its agents.

4.4

The Company, and its directors, officers and agents are not bound to enquire into any title of the transferee of any shares to be transferred, and are not liable to the registered or any intermediate owner of those shares, for registering the transfer.

4.5

There shall be paid to the Company in respect of the registration of any transfer a sum, not exceeding that permitted by the Company Act, as the Directors deem fit.

4.6

The Company may appoint one or more trust Companies as its transfer agent or registrar for the purpose of issuing, countersigning, registering, transferring and certifying the shares and share certificates of the Company and the Company may cause to be kept one or more branch registers of members at such places within or without British Columbia. The directors may from time to time by resolution, regulations or otherwise make such provisions as they think fit respecting the keeping of such registers or branch registers.

PART 5 — TRANSMISSION OF SHARES

5.1

In case of the death of a member, not being one of several joint holders, the representative as set out in the Company Act of the deceased shall be the only person recognized by the Company as having any title to the shares registered in the name of such member, and in the case of death of any one or more of the joint registered holders of any share, the survivor or survivors shall be the only person or persons recognized by the Company as having any title to or interest in such share, but nothing herein contained shall release the estate of a deceased joint holder from any liability in respect of any share that had been jointly held by him with other persons.

5.2

A member's guardian, committee, trustee, curator, tutor, personal representative or Trustee in bankruptcy who becomes entitled to a share as a result of the death or bankruptcy of any member shall, upon production to the registered office of the Company of such documents as may be required by the Company Act be registered as holder of the share to which he is so entitled.

5.3

Any person who becomes entitled to a share by operation of statute or as a result of an order of a court of competent jurisdiction, shall, upon production of such evidence as is required by the Company Act, be registered as holder of such share.

PART 6 — ALTERATION OF CAPITAL

6.1

The Company may, by ordinary resolution filed with the Registrar, amend its memorandum to increase the share capital of the Company by:

    (a)   creating shares with par value or shares without par value, or both;

    (b)   increasing the number of shares with par value or shares without par value, or both;

    (c)   increasing the par value of a class of shares with par value, if no shares of that class are issued.

6.2

The directors may, by resolution, increase the consideration at or for which shares without nominal or par value may be issued.

6.3

Except as otherwise provided by conditions imposed at the time of creation of any new shares or by these Articles, any addition to the authorized capital resulting from the creation of new shares shall be subject to the provisions of these Articles.

6.4

Unless these Articles elsewhere specifically otherwise provide, the provisions of these Articles relating to general meetings shall apply, with the necessary changes and so far as they are applicable, to a class meeting of members holding a particular class of shares. A quorum for a class meeting of members shall be one person holding shares of that class present in person at the commencement of the meeting and representing in person or by proxy not less than one-third of the class of shares affected, and one person, if he is a quorum, may constitute a class meeting.

PART 7 — PURCHASE OF SHARES

7.1

Subject to the special rights and restrictions attached to any class of shares, the Company may, by a resolution of the directors and in compliance with the Company Act, purchase any of its shares at the price and upon the terms specified in such resolution or redeem any class or series of its shares in accordance with the special rights and restrictions attaching thereto. No such purchase or redemption shall be made if the Company is insolvent at the time of the proposed purchase or redemption or if the proposed purchase or redemption would render the Company insolvent. Unless the shares are to be purchased through a stock exchange or unless the Company is purchasing the shares from dissenting members pursuant to the requirements of the Company Act, the Company shall make its offer to purchase pro rata to every member who holds shares of the class to be purchased, unless the purchase is of such a nature that the Company Act exempts such purchase from the requirement of making the offer to purchase pro rata to every member who holds shares of the class or series to be purchased.

7.2

If the company proposes at its option to redeem some but not all of the shares of any class or series, the directors may, subject to the special rights and restrictions attached to such class or series, decide the manner in which the shares to be redeemed shall be selected.

7.3

Subject to the provisions of the Company Act, any shares purchased or redeemed by the Company may be sold or issued by it, but, while such shares are held by the Company, it shall not exercise any vote in respect of these shares and no dividend shall be paid thereon.

PART 8 — BORROWING POWERS

8.1

The directors may from time to time at their discretion authorize the Company to borrow any sum of money for the purposes of the Company and may raise or secure the repayment of that sum in such manner and upon such terms and conditions, in all respects, as they think fit, and in particular, and without limiting the generality of the foregoing, by the issue of bonds or debentures, or any mortgage or charge, whether specific or floating, or other security on the undertaking or the whole or any part of the property of the Company, both present and future.

8.2

The directors may make any debentures, bonds or other debt obligations issued by the Company by their terms, assignable free from any equities between the Company and the person to whom they may be issued, or any other person who lawfully acquires the same by assignment, purchase, or otherwise, howsoever.

8.3

The directors may authorize the issue of any debentures, bonds or other debt obligations of the Company at a discount, premium or otherwise, and with special or other rights or privileges as to redemption, surrender, drawings, allotment of or conversion into or exchange for shares, attending at general meetings of the Company and otherwise as the directors may determine at or before the time of issue.

8.4

The Company shall keep or cause to be kept in accordance with the Company Act:

    (a)   a register of its debentures and debt obligations, and

    (b)   a register of the holders of its bonds, debentures and other debt obligations,

and subject to the provisions, the Company Act may keep or cause to be kept one or more branch registers of the holders of its bonds, debentures, or other debt obligations within or without the Province of British Columbia as the directors may from time to time determine and the directors may by resolution, regulations or otherwise make such provisions as they think fit respecting the keeping of such branch registers.

8.5

If the directors so authorize, or if any instrument under which any bonds, debentures or other debt obligations of the Company are issued so provides, any bonds, debentures and other debt obligations of the Company, instead of being manually signed by the directors or officers authorized in that behalf, may have the facsimile signatures of such directors or officers printed or otherwise mechanically reproduced thereon and in either case, shall be as valid as if signed manually, but no such bond, debenture or other debt obligation shall be issued unless it is manually signed, counter-signed or certified by or on behalf of a trust company or other transfer agent or registrar duly authorized by the directors or the instrument under which such bonds, debentures or other debt obligations are issued so to do. Notwithstanding that any persons whose facsimile signature is so used shall have ceased to hold the office that he is stated on such bond, debenture or other debt obligation to hold at the date of the actual issue thereof, the bond, debenture or other debt obligation shall be valid and binding on the Company.

8.6

Unless the conditions of issue of a debenture otherwise provide, the Company shall, within one month after the allotment of and payment for any debenture, have available for delivery the debenture so allotted and paid for. The Company shall, within one month after the delivery to it of an instrument of transfer of a debenture, have available for delivery the debenture transferred. If the directors of the Company refuse to register a transfer of a debenture, a notice of such refusal shall be sent to the prospective transferee within one month after the date on which the instrument of transfer was delivered to the Company.

PART 9 — GENERAL MEETINGS

9.1

Subject to Article 9.2 and to the Company Act, the first annual general meeting shall be held within 15 months from the date of incorporation and thereafter an annual general meeting shall be held once in every calendar year at such time, not being more than 13 months after the holding of the past preceding annual general meeting, and place as the directors shall appoint. In default of the meeting being so held, the meeting shall be held in the month next following and may be called by any two members in the same manner as nearly as possible as that in which meetings are to be called by the directors.

9.2

If the Company is not a reporting company and if all members entitled to attend and vote at the annual general meeting of the Company consent in writing each year to the business required to be transacted at the annual general meeting, that business shall be as valid as if transacted at an annual general meeting duly convened and held and, it is not necessary for the Company to hold an annual general meeting that year.

9.3

Every general meeting, other than an annual general meeting, shall be called an extraordinary general meeting.

9.4

The directors may, whenever they think fit, and they shall, promptly on the receipt of a requisition of a member or members of the Company representing not less than one-twentieth of such of the issued shares in the capital of the Company as at the date of the requisition carry the right of voting in all circumstances at general meetings, call an extraordinary general meeting of the Company.

9.5

Any such requisition, and the meeting to be called pursuant thereto, shall comply with the provisions of the Company Act.

9.6

Not less than 21 days' notice of any general meeting specifying the time and place of meeting and in case of special business, the general nature of that business shall be given in the manner mentioned in Article 21, or in such other manner, if any, as may be prescribed by ordinary resolution whether previous notice thereof has been given or not, to any person as may by law or under these Articles or other regulations of the Company entitled to receive such notice from the Company. But the accidental omission to give notice of any meeting to, or the non-receipt of any such notice by, any of such persons shall not invalidate any proceedings at that meeting.

9.7

All the members of the Company entitled to attend at a general meeting may, by unanimous consent in writing given before, during or after the meeting, or, if they are present at the meeting by a unanimous vote, waive or reduce the period of notice of such meeting, and an entry in the minute book of such waiver or reduction shall be sufficient evidence of the due convening of the meeting. The directors may, for the purpose of determining members entitled to notice of, or to vote at, any general meeting or class meeting fix in advance a date as the record date, which date shall not be more than 49 days before the date of the meeting. Where no such record date is fixed, it shall be deemed to be the date on which the notice calling the general meeting or class meeting is mailed for the purpose of determining those members entitled to notice and to vote at such meeting.

9.8

Where any special business includes the presenting, considering, approving, ratifying or authorizing of the execution of any document, then the portion of any notice relating to such document shall be sufficient if the same states that a copy of the document or proposed document is or will be available for inspection by members at a place in the Province of British Columbia specified in such notice during business hours in any specified working day or days prior to the date of the meeting.

PART 10 — PROCEEDINGS AT GENERAL MEETINGS

10.1

The following business at a general meeting shall be deemed to be special business:

(a) all business at an extraordinary general meeting, and

(b) all business that is transacted at an annual general meeting, with the exception of the consideration of the financial statement and the report of the directors and auditors, the election of directors, the appointment of the auditors and such other business as, under these Articles, ought to be transacted at an annual general meeting, or any business which is brought under consideration by the report of the directors.

10.2

Save as otherwise herein provided a quorum for a general meeting shall be:

(a) two members or proxyholders representing two members; or

(b) one member and a proxyholder representing another member

personally present at the commencement of the meeting and holding or representing by proxy not less than one-twentieth of the issued shares of a class of shares the holders of which are entitled to attend and to vote at such meeting. Where the Company has only one member, the quorum shall be that member or his proxyholder.

10.3

No business, other than the election of a chairman and the adjournment of the meeting shall be transacted at any general meeting unless the quorum requisite is present at the commencement of the meeting, but such quorum need not be present throughout the meeting.

10.4

If within one-half hour from the time appointed for a meeting, a quorum is not present, the meeting, if convened by requisition of the members, shall be dissolved; but in any other case it shall stand adjourned to the same day in the next week at the same time and place. If at such adjourned meeting a quorum is not present within one-half hour from the time appointed, the person or persons present and being or representing by proxy, a member or members entitled to attend and vote at the meeting shall constitute a quorum.

10.5

The Chairman of the Board, if any, or in his absence the President of the Company shall be entitled to preside as chairman at every general meeting of the Company.

10.6

If at any meeting neither the Chairman of the Board, if any, nor the President is present within fifteen minutes after the time appointed for holding the meeting or is willing to act as chairman, the directors present shall choose some one of their number to be chairman. If no director be present or if all the directors present decline to take the chair or shall fail to so choose, the members present shall choose one of their number to be chairman.

10.7

The chairman of the meeting may, with the consent of any meeting at which a quorum is present and shall if so directed by the meeting, adjourn the meeting from time to time and from place to place, but no business shall be transacted at any adjourned meeting other than the business left unfinished at the meeting from which the adjournment took place. When a meeting is adjourned for 30 days or more, notice of the adjourned meeting shall be given as in the case of a general meeting. Save as aforesaid, it shall not be necessary to give any notice of an adjournment or of the business to be transacted at an adjourned meeting.

10.8

Subject to the provisions of the Company Act, every question submitted to a general meeting shall be decided on a show of hands unless a poll is, before or on the declaration of the result of the show of hands, directed by the chairman or demanded by a member entitled to vote who is present in person or by proxy, and the chairman shall declare to the meeting the decision on every question in accordance with the result of the show of hands or the poll, and such decision shall be entered in the book of proceedings of the Company. A declaration by the chairman that a resolution has been carried or carried unanimously or by a particular majority, or lost or not carried by a particular majority, and an entry to that effect in the book containing the minutes of the proceedings of the Company shall be conclusive evidence of the fact without proof of the number or proportion of the votes recorded in favour of or against such resolution.

10.9

No resolution proposed at a meeting need be seconded and the chairman of any meeting shall be entitled to move or second a resolution.

10.10

In case of an equality of votes upon a resolution the chairman shall *not*, either on a show of hands or on a poll, have a casting or second vote in addition to the vote or votes to which he may be entitled as a member.

10.11

Subject to the provisions of Article 10.13, if a poll is duly demanded as aforesaid, it shall be taken in such manner and at such time within seven days from the date of the meeting and place as the chairman of the meeting directs, and either at once or after an interval or adjournment not exceeding seven days, and the result of the poll shall be deemed to be the resolution of the meeting at which the poll is demanded. A demand for a poll may be withdrawn. In the case of any dispute as to the admission or rejection of a vote, the chairman shall determine the same and such determination made in good faith shall be final and conclusive.

10.12

A member entitled to more than one vote need not, if he votes, use all his votes or cast all the votes he uses in the same way.

10.13

No poll may be demanded on the election of a chairman of a meeting and a poll demanded on a question of adjournment shall be taken at the meeting without adjournment.

10.14

The demand of a poll shall not prevent the continuance of a meeting for the transaction of any business other than the question on which a poll has been demanded.

10.15

Every ballot cast upon a poll and every proxy appointing a proxyholder who cast a ballot upon a poll shall be retained by the Secretary for the period and be subject to the inspection as the Company Act may provide.

PART 11 — VOTES OF MEMBERS

11.1

Subject to any special rights or restrictions for the time being attached to any shares, on a show of hands every member present in person shall have one vote, and on a poll every member, present in person or by proxy, shall have one vote for each share which is registered in his name.

11.2

Any person who is not registered as a member but is entitled to vote at any general meeting in respect of a share, may vote the share in the same manner as if he were a member; but, unless the directors have previously admitted his right to vote at that meeting in respect of the share, he shall satisfy the directors of his right to vote the share before the time for holding the meeting, or adjourned meeting, as the case may be, at which he proposes to vote.

11.3

Where there are joint members registered in respect of any share, any one of the joint members may vote at any meeting, either personally or by proxy, in respect of the share as if he were solely entitled to it. If more than one of the joint members is present at any meeting, personally or by proxy, the joint member present whose name stands first on the register in respect of the share shall alone be entitled to vote in respect of that share. Several executors or administrators of a deceased member in whose sole name any share stands shall, for the purpose of this Article, be deemed joint members.

11.4

A corporation, not being a subsidiary of the Company, that is a member may vote by its proxyholder or by its duly authorized representative. Such proxyholder or duly authorized representative is entitled to speak, vote, and in all other respects exercise the rights of a member and shall be deemed to be a member for all purposes in connection with any general meeting of the Company. Where the member is a subsidiary of the Company, the member shall not form part of the quorum, or vote or permit to be voted any shares of the Company registered in its name at a general meeting of members of the Company.

11.5

A member for whom a committee has been duly appointed may vote, whether on a show of hands or on a poll, by his committee and his committee may appoint a proxyholder.

11.6

A member holding more than one share in respect of which he is entitled to vote shall be entitled to appoint one or more proxyholders to attend, act and vote for him on the same occasion. If such a member should appoint more than one proxyholder for the same occasion, he shall specify the number of shares each proxyholder shall be entitled to vote.

11.7

A proxy or an instrument appointing a duly authorized representative of a corporation shall be in writing, under the hand of the appointor or of his attorney duly authorized in writing, or, if such appointor is a corporation, either under its seal or under the hand of an officer or attorney duly authorized.

11.8

A proxyholder need not be a member of the Company if:

    (a)   the Company is at the time a reporting company, or

    (b)   the member appointing the proxyholder is a corporation, or

    (c)   the Company shall have at the time only one member, or

    (d)   the persons present in person or by proxy and entitled to vote at the meeting by resolution permit the proxyholder to attend and vote; for the purpose of such resolution the proxyholder shall be counted in the quorum but shall not be entitled to vote,

and in all other cases a proxyholder must be a member of the Company.

11.9

A proxy and the power of attorney or other authority, if any, under which it is signed or a notarially certified copy thereof shall be deposited at the registered office of the Company or at such other place as is specified for that purpose in the notice calling the meeting, not less than 48 hours before the time for holding the meeting at which the person named in the proxy proposes to vote, or shall be deposited with the chairman of the meeting prior to the commencement thereof. In addition to any other method of depositing proxies provided for in these Articles, the directors may from time to time make regulations permitting the lodgings of proxies appointing proxyholders at some place or places other than the place at which a meeting or adjourned meeting of members is to be held and for particulars of such proxies to be cabled or telegraphed or sent in writing before the meeting or adjourned meeting to the Company or any agent of the Company for the purpose of receiving such particulars and providing that proxies appointing a proxyholder so lodged may be voted upon as though the proxies themselves were produced to the chairman of the meeting or adjourned meeting as required by this part and votes given in accordance with such regulations shall be valid and shall be counted.

11.10

A vote given in accordance with the terms of a proxy shall be valid notwithstanding the previous death or insanity of the member or revocation of the proxy or of the authority under which the proxy was executed, or the transfer of the share in respect of which the proxy is given, provided no prior notice in writing of the death, insanity, revocation or transfer as aforesaid shall have been received at the registered office of the Company or by the chairman of the meeting or adjourned meeting at which the vote was given.

11.11

Unless, in the circumstances, the Company Act requires any other form of proxy, a proxy appointing a proxyholder, whether for a specified meeting or otherwise, shall be in the form following, or in any other form that the directors shall approve:

(Name of Company)*

The undersigned hereby appoints _____
(or failing him _____
of _____), as pro holder for the undersigned to attend at
and vote for and on behalf of the undersigned at the general meeting of the Company to be held on the _____
day of _____, 20 _____ and at any adjournment of that meeting.

Signed this _____ day of _____, 20 _____ .

_____
(Signature of Member)

PART 12 — DIRECTORS

12.1

The management of the business of the company shall be vested in the directors and the directors may exercise all such powers and do all such acts and things as the Company is, by its Memorandum or otherwise, authorized to exercise and do, and which are not by these Articles or by statute or otherwise lawfully directed or required to be exercised or done by the Company in general meeting, but subject nevertheless to the provisions of all laws affecting the Company and of these Articles and to any regulations not being inconsistent with these Articles which shall from time to time be made by the Company in general meeting; but no regulation made by the Company in general meeting shall invalidate any prior act of the directors that would have been valid if that regulation had not been made.

12.2

The subscriber(s) to the Memorandum are the first directors. The directors to succeed the first directors and the number of directors may be determined in writing by a majority of the subscribers to the Memorandum. The number of directors may be changed from time to time by ordinary resolution, whether previous notice thereof has been given or not, but shall never be less than one while the Company is not a reporting company and three while the Company is a reporting company.

12.3

A director shall not be required to have any share qualification but any person not being a member of the Company who becomes a director shall be deemed to have agreed to be bound by the provisions of the Articles to the same extent as if he were a member of the Company.

*Note: Do not fill in the sample proxy on your copy of these articles.

12.4

The remuneration of the directors as such may from time to time be determined by the members, unless by ordinary resolution the directors are authorized to determine their remuneration. Such remuneration is to be in addition to any salary or other remuneration paid to any officer or employee of the Company as such, who is also a director. The directors shall be repaid such reasonable expenses as they may incur in and about the business of the Company and if any director shall perform any professional or other services for the Company that in the opinion of the directors are outside the ordinary duties of a director or shall otherwise be specifically occupied in or about the Company's business, he may be paid a remuneration to be fixed by the Board, or, at the option of such director, by the Company in general meeting, and such remuneration may be either in addition to, or in substitution for, any other remuneration that he may be entitled to receive, and the same shall be charged as part of the ordinary working expenses. Unless otherwise determined by ordinary resolution, the directors on behalf of the Company may pay a gratuity or pension or allowance on retirement to any director who has held any salaried office or place of profit with the Company or to his spouse or dependants and may make contributions to any fund and pay premiums for the purchase or provision of any such gratuity, pension or allowance.

12.5

The directors may from time to time and at any time by power of attorney appoint any company, firm or person or body of persons, whether nominated directly or indirectly by the directors, to be the attorney or attorneys of the Company for such purposes and with such powers, authorities and discretions, not exceeding those vested in or exercisable by the directors under these Articles, and for such period and subject to such conditions as they may think fit, and any such powers of attorney may contain such provisions for the protection and convenience of persons dealing with any such attorney as the directors may think fit and may also authorize any such attorney to delegate all or any of the powers, authorities and discretions vested in him.

12.6

A director who is in any way, whether directly or indirectly, interested in a contract or proposed contract or arrangement with the Company shall declare the nature of his interest at a meeting of the directors in accordance with the provisions of the Company Act. A director shall not vote in respect of any such contract or transaction with the Company in which he is interested and if he shall do so his vote shall not be counted, but he may be counted in the quorum present at the meeting at which such vote is taken. Subject to the Company Act, the foregoing shall not apply to:

(a)   any contract or transaction relating to a loan to the company, which a director or a specified corporation or a specified firm in which he has an interest has guaranteed or joined in guaranteeing the repayment of the loan or any part of the loan, or

(b)   any contract or transaction made or to be made with, or for the benefit of an affiliated corporation of which a director is a director or officer, or

(c)   determining the remuneration of the directors, or

(d)   purchasing and maintaining insurance to cover directors against liability incurred by them as directors, or

(e)   the indemnification of any director by the Company.

Subject to the Company Act, the foregoing prohibitions and exceptions thereto may from time to time be suspended or amended to any extent by ordinary resolution, either generally or in respect of any particular contract, arrangement or transaction or for any particular period.

12.7

A director may hold any office or place of profit under the Company, other than auditor, in conjunction with his office of director for such period and on such period and on such terms, as to remuneration or otherwise, as the directors may determine. Subject to compliance with the Company Act, no director or intended director shall be disqualified by his office from contracting with the office or place of profit or as vendor, purchaser or otherwise, and, subject to compliance with the Company Act, no contract or transaction entered into by or on behalf of the Company in which a director is in any way interested shall be liable to be avoided.

12.8

Any director may act by himself or his firm in a professional capacity for the Company, and he or his firm shall be entitled to remuneration for professional services as if he were not a director.

12.9

A director may be or become a director or other officer or employee of, or otherwise interested in, any corporation or firm in which the Company may be interested as a shareholder or otherwise, and, subject to compliance with the provisions of the Company Act, such director shall not be accountable to the Company for any remuneration or other benefits received by him as director, officer or employee of, or from his interest in, such other corporation or firm, unless the Company in general meeting otherwise directs.

12.10

Any director may, from time to time, appoint any person who is approved by resolution of the directors to be his alternate director. The appointee, while he holds office as an alternate director, shall be entitled to notice of meetings of the directors and, in the absence of the director for whom he is an alternate, to attend and vote thereat as a director or sign any resolution of directors to be consented to in writing, and shall not be entitled to be remunerated otherwise than out of the remuneration of the director appointing him. Any director may make or revoke an appointment of his alternate director by notice in writing or by telegram or cable to be delivered or addressed, postage or other charges prepaid, to the registered office of the Company. The directors may by resolution revoke any appointment of an alternate director, any such revocation to become effective upon notice thereof having been given to the director who made the appointment. No person shall act as an alternate for more than one director at any given time and no director may act as an alternate for any other director.

PART 13 — TERMINATION OF DIRECTORSHIP OF DIRECTORS

13.1

The directorship of a director shall be immediately terminated:

(a) if by notice in writing to the Company at its registered office he resigns;

(b) if he is removed pursuant to Article 14.2;

(c) if convicted within or without the Province of an indictable offence and the other directors resolve to remove him; or

(d) if he ceases to be qualified to act as a director under the Company Act.

PART 14 — RETIREMENT AND ELECTION OF DIRECTORS

14.1

At each annual general meeting of the Company all the directors shall retire and the Company shall elect a Board of Directors consisting of the number of directors for the time being fixed pursuant to these Articles. If in any calendar year the Company does not hold an annual general meeting, the directors appointed at the last annual general meeting of the Company shall be deemed to have been elected or appointed as directors on the last day on which the meeting could have been held pursuant to the Company Act and the directors so appointed or elected may hold office until other directors are appointed or elected or until the day on which the next annual general meeting is held.

14.2

The Company may by special resolution remove any director and, by ordinary resolution, appoint another person in his stead. Any director so appointed shall hold office only until the next following annual general meeting of the Company, but shall be eligible for re-election at such meeting.

14.3

The directors shall have power at any time and from time to time to appoint any person as a director, to fill a casual vacancy on the Board or a vacancy resulting from an increase of the number of directors necessitated by the Company Act upon the Company becoming a reporting company. Any director so appointed shall hold office only until the next following annual general meeting of the Company, but shall be eligible for re-election at such meeting.

PART 15 — PROCEEDINGS OF DIRECTORS

15.1

The directors may meet together at such places as they think fit for the dispatch of business, adjourn and otherwise regulate their meetings and proceedings, as they see fit. The directors may from time to time fix the quorum necessary for the transaction of business and unless so fixed such quorum shall be a majority of the Board. The Chairman of the Board, if any, or in his absence the President of the Company, shall be chairman of all meetings of the Board, but if at any meeting neither the Chairman of the Board, if any, nor the President shall be present within 15 minutes after the time appointed for holding the same or if both the Chairman of the Board and the President, being present decline to act, the directors present may choose some one of their number to be chairman at such meeting. A director interested is to be counted in a quorum notwithstanding his interest. In the event the Company is a one-man company, a quorum shall consist of one.

15.2

A director may at any time, and the Secretary shall, upon the written request of a director, call a meeting of the directors. Reasonable notice thereof specifying the time and place of such meeting shall be mailed, postage prepaid, addressed to each of the directors at his registered address before the time fixed for the meeting or such notice may be given to each director either personally or by leaving it at his usual business or residential address or by telephone, telegram, telex or other method of transmitting visually recorded messages. It shall not be necessary to give to any director notice of a meeting of directors immediately following a general meeting at which such director has been elected or notice of a meeting of directors at which such director shall have been appointed. Accidental omission to give notice of a meeting of directors to, or the non-receipt of notice by, any director, shall not invalidate the proceedings at that meeting.

15.3

A meeting of the directors at which a quorum is present shall be competent to exercise all or any of the authorities, power and discretion for the time being vested in or exercisable by the directors.

15.4

The continuing directors may act notwithstanding any vacancy in their body, but, if and so long as their number is reduced below the number fixed pursuant to these Articles as the necessary quorum of directors, the continuing directors or director may act for the purpose of filling vacancies increasing the number of directors to that number, or for the purpose of summoning a general meeting of the Company, but for no other purpose.

15.5

The directors may delegate any but not all of their powers to committees consisting of such of the directors as they think fit. Any committee so formed shall in the exercise of the powers so delegated conform to any regulations that may from time to time be imposed on it by the directors, and shall keep regular minutes of their transactions and shall cause such minutes to be recorded in books kept for that purpose, and shall report the same to the Board of Directors at such times as the Board shall require.

15.6

A committee may elect a chairman of its meetings; if no such chairman is elected, or if at any meetings the chairman is not present within 15 minutes after the time appointed for holding the same, the members present may choose one of their number to be chairman of the meeting.

15.7

The members of a committee may meet and adjourn as they think proper. Questions arising at any meeting shall be determined by a majority of votes of the members present and in case of an equality of votes the chairman shall not have a second or casting vote.

15.8

All acts done by any meeting of the directors or by a committee of directors or by any person acting as a director shall, notwithstanding that it shall be afterwards discovered that there was some defect in the appointment of any such director or person acting as aforesaid, or that they or any of them were disqualified, be as valid as if every such person had been duly appointed and was qualified to be a director.

15.9

For the first meeting of the Board to be held immediately following the appointment or election of a director or directors at an annual or general meeting of shareholders or for a meeting of the Board at which a director is appointed to fill a vacancy in the Board, no notice of such meetings shall be necessary to the newly elected or appointed director or directors in order for the meeting to be duly constituted, provided that a quorum of directors is present.

15.10

Any director of the Company who may be absent either temporarily or permanently from the Province of British Columbia may file at the office of the Company a waiver of notice which may be by letter, telegram or cable of any meeting of the directors and may at any time withdraw such waiver, and until such waiver is withdrawn, no notice of meetings of directors shall be sent to such director, and any and all meetings of the directors of the Company, notice of which shall not have been given to such director, shall, provided a quorum of the directors is present, be valid and binding upon the Company.

15.11

Questions arising at any meeting of the directors shall be decided by a majority of votes. In case of an equality of votes, the Chairman shall not have a second or casting vote.

15.12

A resolution consented to in writing, whether by document, telegram, telex or any method of transmitting legibly recorded messages by all of the directors shall be as valid and effectual as if it had been passed at a meeting of the directors duly called and held. Such resolution may be in two or more counterparts which together shall be deemed to constitute one resolution in writing. Such resolution shall be filed with the minutes of the proceedings of the directors and shall be effective on the dates stated therein or the latest date stated on any counterparts.

15.13

A director may participate in a meeting of the Board or of any committee of the directors through the use of conference telephones or other communication facilities by means of which all directors participating in the meeting can hear each other and provided that all such directors agree to such participation. A director participating in a meeting in accordance with this Article shall be deemed to be present at the meeting and to have so agreed and shall be counted in the quorum therefore and be entitled to speak and vote threat.

PART 16 — OFFICERS

16.1

The Board of Directors shall from time to time appoint a President and a Secretary and may appoint such other officers of the Company as it may determine, none of whom, save the Chairman of the Board, if any, and the President, need be directors. Such officers shall be qualified pursuant to the Company Act to hold office. One person may hold more than one of such offices except that the offices of President and Secretary must be held by different persons unless the Company has only one member.

16.2

All appointments of officers shall be made upon such terms and conditions and at such remuneration, whether by way of salary, fee, commission, participation in profits, or otherwise, as the directors may determine, and every such appointment shall be subject to termination at the pleasure of the directors unless otherwise fixed by contract.

16.3

Every officer of the Company who holds any office or possesses any property whereby, whether directly or indirectly, duties or interests might be created in conflict with his duties or interests as an officer of the Company shall, in writing, disclose to the President the fact and nature, character and extent of the conflict.

16.4

The Secretary of the Company shall:

(a) keep or cause to be kept the records of the Company in accordance with the provisions of the Company Act;

(b) make or cause to be made all required filings with the Registrar of Companies for the Province of British Columbia, including the filing within 14 days of being passed, a certified copy of every resolution which by the Company Act does not take effect until such filing has been made; and

(c) perform such other duties as may be assigned to the office.

PART 17 — MINUTES, DOCUMENTS AND RECORDS

17.1

The directors shall cause minutes to be duly entered in books provided for the purposes:

(a) of all appointments of officers;

(b) of the names of the directors or their alternates present at each meeting of directors and of any committee of directors;

(c) of all orders made by the directors or committees of directors;

(d) of all resolutions and proceedings of general meetings of the Company and of all meetings of the directors and of committees of directors;

(e) of all waivers signed or resolutions passed by consent being given thereto in writing.

17.2

The directors shall cause the Company to keep at its records office or at such other place as the Company Act may permit, the documents, copy documents, registers, minutes, and records which the Company is required by the Company Act to keep at its records office or such other place.

PART 18 — EXECUTION OF DOCUMENTS

18.1

The directors may provide a common seal for the company and for its use and the directors shall have power from time to time to destroy the same and substitute a new seal in place thereof.

18.2

Subject to the provisions of the Company Act, the directors may provide for use in any other Province, Territory, State or Country an official seal, which shall have on its face the name of the Province, Territory, State or Country where it is to be used.

18.3

If the Company has a common seal, the directors shall provide for its safe custody and it shall not be impressed on any instrument except when such impression is attested by the signature or signatures of:

(a) the President, a Vice-President or director, together with the Secretary or an Assistant Secretary; or

(b) any two directors; or

(c) such one or more directors or officers as may be prescribed from time to time by resolution of the directors; or

(d) where the company has but one director, that director or the Secretary or an Assistant Secretary.

18.4

The signature of any officer of the Company may, if authorized by the directors, be printed, lithographed, engraved or otherwise mechanically reproduced upon all instruments executed or issued by the Company or any officer thereof; and any instrument on which the signature of any such person is so reproduced shall be deemed to have been manually signed by such person whose signature is so reproduced and shall be as valid to all intents and purposes as if such instrument had been signed manually, and notwithstanding that the person whose signature is so reproduced may have ceased to hold office at the date of the delivery or issue of such instrument. The term "instrument" as used in this Article shall include deeds, mortgages, hypothecs, charges, conveyances, transfers and assignments of property, real or personal, agreements releases, receipts and discharges for the payment of money or other obligations, certificates of the Company's shares, share warrants of the Company, bonds, debentures and other debt obligations of the Company, and all paper writings.

PART 19 — DIVIDENDS

19.1

The directors may declare dividends and fix the date of record therefore and the date for payment thereof. No notice need be given of the declaration of any dividend. If no date of record is fixed, the date of record shall be deemed to be the same date as the date the dividend is declared. No dividend shall be paid otherwise than out of funds and/or assets properly available for the payment of dividends and a declaration by the directors as to the sufficiency of such funds and/or assets available for dividends shall be conclusive.

19.2

Subject to the terms of shares with special rights or restrictions, all dividends shall be declared according to the number of shares held.

19.3

No dividend shall bear interest against the Company. Where the dividend to which a member is entitled includes a fraction of a cent, such fraction shall be disregarded in making payment thereof and such payment shall be deemed to be payment in full.

19.4

The directors may direct payment of any dividend wholly or partly by the distribution of specific assets or of paid-up shares, bonds, debentures or other debt obligations of the Company, or in any one or more of these ways, and, where any difficulty arises in regard to the distribution, the directors may settle the same as they think expedient, and in particular may fix the value for distribution of specific assets, and may determine that cash payments shall be made to a member upon the basis of the value so fixed in place of fractional shares, bonds, debentures or other debt obligations in order to adjust the rights of all parties, and may vest any of those specific assets in trustees upon such trusts for the persons entitled as may seem expedient to the directors.

19.5

Notwithstanding anything contained in these Articles, the directors may from time to time capitalize any undistributed surplus on hand of the Company and may from time to time issue as fully paid and non-assessable any unissued shares or any bonds, debentures or other debt obligations of the Company as a dividend representing such undistributed surplus on hand or any part thereof.

19.6

Any dividend, interest or other monies payable in cash in respect of shares may be paid by cheque or warrant sent through the post directed to the registered address of the holder, or, in the case of joint holders, to the registered address of that one of the joint holders who is first named on the register or to such person and to such address as the holder or joint holders may in writing direct. Every such cheque or warrant shall be made payable to the order of the person to whom it is sent. Any one of two or more joint holders may give effectual receipts for any dividends, bonuses or other monies payable in respect of the shares held by them as joint holders, and the Company is not bound to see to the execution of any trust in respect of shares of the Company. The mailing of such cheque or warrant shall, to the extent of the sum represented thereby (plus the amount of any tax required by law to be deducted) discharge all liability for the dividend, unless such cheque or warrant shall not be paid on presentation or the amount of tax so deducted is not paid to the appropriate taxing authority.

19.7

No dividend shall be paid if:

    (a)   the Company is insolvent; or

    (b)   the payment of the dividend would render the Company insolvent; or

(c) the Company has outstanding shares containing rights which provide that those shares shall be redeemed or purchased on or before a certain date and provision has not been made for a capital redemption fund in compliance with the Company Act.

19.8

A transfer of a share shall not pass the right to any dividend declared thereon before the registration of the transfer in the register.

19.9

Notwithstanding any other provisions of these Articles should any dividend result in any shareholders being entitled to a fractional part of a share of the Company, the directors shall have the right to pay such shareholders in place of that fractional share, the cash equivalent thereof calculated on the par value thereof or, in the case of shares without nominal or par value, calculated on the price or consideration for which such shares were or were deemed to be issued, and shall have the further right and complete discretion to carry out such distribution and to adjust the rights of the shareholders with respect thereto on as practical and equitable a basis as possible including the right to arrange through a fiscal agent or otherwise for the sale, consolidation or other disposition of those fractional shares on behalf of those shareholders of the Company.

19.10

The directors may, before declaring any dividend, set aside out of the profits of the Company such sums as they think proper as appropriations from income, which shall at the discretion of the directors, be applicable for meeting contingencies, or for equalizing dividends, or for any other purpose to which the profits of the company may be properly applied, and pending such application may, either be employed in the business of the Company or be invested in such investments as the directors in their discretion may from time to time determine.

PART 20 — ACCOUNTS

20.1

The directors shall cause records and books of accounts to be kept as necessary to properly record the financial affairs and conditions of the Company and to comply with the provisions of statutes applicable to the Company.

20.2

The directors shall determine the place at which the accounting records of the Company shall be kept and those records shall be open to the inspection of any director during the normal business hours of the Company.

20.3

The directors shall determine to what extent, at what times and places and under what conditions the accounting records of the Company shall be open to the inspection of members.

PART 21 — NOTICES

21.1

In this Part 21, unless the context otherwise requires, the word notice shall include a notice, statement, report or any other document.

21.2

In addition to any other method of giving notice as set out in the Company Act, or as otherwise set out in these Articles, a notice may be given or delivered to any member or director, either personally or by sending it by post to him in a letter, envelope or wrapper, postage prepaid, addressed to the member or director at his registered address. A certificate signed by the Secretary or other officer of the Company or of any other corporation acting in that behalf for the Company that the letter, envelope or wrapper containing the notice, statement or report was so addressed, prepaid and mailed shall be conclusive evidence thereof.

21.3

A notice may be given by the Company to joint members in respect of a share registered in their names by giving the notice to the joint member first named in the register of members in respect of that share.

21.4

A notice may be given by the Company to the persons entitled to a share in consequence of the death or bankruptcy of a member by sending it through the post in a prepaid letter, envelope or wrapper addressed to them by name, or by the title of representatives of the deceased, or trustee of the bankrupt, or by any like description, at the address, if any, supplied for the purpose by the persons claiming to be so entitled, or until that address has been so supplied, by giving the notice in any manner in which the same might have been given if the death or bankruptcy had not occurred.

21.5

Any notice or document sent by post to or left at the registered address of any member shall, notwithstanding that member is then deceased and whether or not the Company has notice of his death, be deemed to have been duly served in respect of any registered shares, whether held solely or jointly with other persons by that deceased member, until some other person is registered in his place as the member or joint member in respect of those shares, and that service shall for all purposes of these Articles be deemed a sufficient service of such notice or document on his personal representatives and all persons, if any, jointly interested with him in those shares.

21.6

Any notice sent by post shall be deemed to have been served on the day following that on which the letter, envelope or wrapper containing that notice is posted, and in proving service thereof it shall be sufficient to prove that the letter, envelope or wrapper containing the notice was properly addressed and put in a Canadian Government post office, postage prepaid.

21.7

If a number of days' notice or a notice extending over any other period is required to be given, the day of service shall not, unless it is otherwise provided in these Articles, be counted in the number of days or other period required.

21.8

Notice of every general meeting shall be given in the manner authorized by these Articles, to:

    (a)   every member holding a share or shares carrying the right to vote at such meetings on the record date or, if no record date was established by the directors, on the date of mailing;

    (b)   the personal representative of a deceased member;

    (c)   the trustee in bankruptcy of a bankrupt member; and

    (d)   the auditor of the Company, if any.

PART 22 — INDEMNIFICATION AND PROTECTION OF DIRECTORS, OFFICERS, EMPLOYEES, AND CERTAIN AGENTS

22.1

The Company shall indemnify any person who was or is a party or is threatened to be made a party to any threatened, pending or completed action or proceeding, whether or not brought by the Company or by a corporation or other legal entity or enterprise, officer, employee, or agent of the Company or is or was serving at the request of the Company as a director, officer, employee or agent of another corporation, a partnership, joint venture, trust or other enterprise, against all costs, charges and expenses, including legal fees and any amount paid to settle the action or proceeding or satisfy a judgment, if he acted honestly and in good faith with a view to the best interests of the corporation or other legal entity or enterprise as aforesaid of which he is or was a director, officer, employee or agent, as the case may be, and exercised the care, diligence and skill of a reasonably prudent person, and with respect to any criminal or administrative action or proceeding, he had reasonable grounds for believing that his conduct was lawful; provided that no one shall be indemnified hereunder:

    (a)   if he has failed to carry out his duty to act in accordance with the Company Act or any rule of law; and in any event,

      (b)   until court approval has been granted with respect to such indemnification.

The determination of any action, suit or proceeding by judgment, order, settlement, conviction or otherwise shall not, of itself, create a presumption that the person did not act honestly and in good faith and in the best interests of the Company and did not exercise the care, diligence and skill of a reasonably prudent person and, with respect to any criminal action or proceeding, did not have reasonable grounds to believe that his conduct was lawful.

22.2

The Company shall indemnify any person other than a director in respect of any loss, damage, costs or expenses whatsoever incurred by him while acting as an officer, employee or agent for the Company unless such loss, damage, costs or expenses shall arise out of failure to comply with instructions, wilful act or default or fraud by such person in any of which events the Company shall only indemnify such person if the directors, in their absolute discretion, so decide or the Company by ordinary resolution shall so direct.

22.3

The indemnification provided by this Part shall not be deemed exclusive of any other rights to which those seeking indemnification may be entitled under any other Part, or any valid and lawful agreement, vote of members or disinterested directors or otherwise, both as to action in his official capacity and as to action in another capacity while holding such office, and shall continue as to a person who has ceased to be a director, officer, employee or agent and shall ensure to the benefit of the heirs, executors and administrators of such person. The indemnification provided by this Article shall not be exclusive of any powers, rights, agreements or undertakings which may be legally permissible or authorized by or under any applicable law. Notwithstanding any other provisions set forth in this Part, the indemnification authorized by this Part shall be applicable only to the extent that any such indemnification shall not duplicate indemnity or reimbursement which that person has received or shall receive otherwise than under this Part.

22.4

The directors are authorized from time to time to cause the Company to give indemnities to any director, officer, employee, agent or other person who has undertaken or is about to undertake any liability on behalf of the Company or any corporation controlled by it. The failure of a director or officer of the Company to comply with the provisions of the Company Act, the Memorandum or these Articles shall not invalidate any indemnity to which he is entitled under this Part.

22.5

Subject to the Company Act, no director or officer or employee for the time being of the Company shall be liable for the acts, receipts, neglects or defaults of any other director or officer or employee, or for joining in any receipt or act for conformity, or for any loss, damage or expense happening to the Company through the insufficiency or deficiency of any security in or upon which any of the monies of or belonging to the Company shall be invested or for any loss or damages arising from the bankruptcy, insolvency, or tortious act of any person, firm or corporation with whom or which any monies, securities or effects shall be lodged or deposited or for any loss occasioned by any error of judgment or oversight on his part or for any other loss, damage or misfortune whatever which may happen in the execution of the duties of his respective office or trust or in relation thereto unless the same shall happen by or through his own wilful act or default, negligence, breach of trust or breach of duty.

22.6

Directors may rely upon the accuracy of any statement of fact represented by an officer of the Company to be correct or upon statements in a written report of the auditor of the Company and shall not be responsible or held liable for any loss or damage resulting from the paying of any dividends or otherwise acting in good faith upon any such statement.

22.7

The directors may cause the Company to purchase and maintain insurance for the benefit of any person who is or was a director, officer, employee or agent of the Company or is or was serving at the request of the Company as a director, officer, employee or agent of another corporation, a partnership, joint venture, trust or other enterprise and his heirs and representatives against any liability incurred by him as a director, officer, employee or agent.

PART 23 — PROHIBITIONS

23.1

No transfer of shares shall be entered in the register of members without the prior approval of the majority of directors, and the Company shall not keep a branch register of members outside the Province of British Columbia unless the Company Act so permits.

PART 24 — RESTRICTIONS ON SHARE TRANSFERS

24.1

Notwithstanding anything contained in these Articles the directors may in their absolute discretion decline to register any transfer of shares and shall not be required to disclose their reasons therefor; provided that at such time as the securities of the Company have been listed for trading on any stock exchange or any regulatory authority has accepted for filing and has issued a receipt for a prospectus qualifying the distribution of the Company's securities to the public, any restriction on the transfer of shares of the Company shall, by that fact, be removed.

24.2

No shares in the capital of the Company shall be transferred by any member, or the personal representative of any deceased member or trustee in bankruptcy of any bankrupt member, or the liquidator of a member which is a corporation, except under the following conditions.

(a) A person (herein called the "proposing transferor") desiring to transfer any share or shares in the Company shall give notice in writing (herein called the "transfer notice") to the Company that he desires to transfer the same. The transfer notice shall specify the price, which shall be expressed in lawful money of Canada, and the terms of payment upon which the proposing transferor is prepared to transfer the share or shares and shall constitute the Company his agent for the sale thereof to any member or members of the Company at the price and upon the terms of payment so specified. The transfer notice shall also state whether or not the proposing transferor has had an offer to purchase the shares or any of them from, or proposes to sell the shares or any of them to, any particular person or persons who are not members and if so the names and addresses of such persons shall be specified in the transfer notice. The transfer notice shall constitute an offer by the proposing transferor to the other members of the Company holding shares of the class or classes included in the transfer notice and shall not be revocable except with the sanction of the directors. If the transfer notice pertains to shares of more than one class, then the consideration and terms of payment for each class of shares shall be stated separately in the transfer notice.

(b) The directors shall forthwith upon receipt thereof transmit the transfer notice to each of the members, other than the proposing transferor, holding shares of the class or classes set forth in the transfer notice and request the member to whom the transfer notice is sent to state in writing within 14 days from the date of the transfer notice whether he is willing to accept any, and if so, the maximum number of shares he is willing to accept at the price and upon the terms specified in the transfer notice. A member shall only be entitled to purchase shares of the class or classes held by him.

(c) Upon the expiration of the 14-day notice period referred to in Article 24.2 (b), if the directors shall have received from the members entitled to receive the transfer notice sufficient acceptances to take up the full number of shares offered by the transfer notice and, if the transfer notice includes shares of more than one class, sufficient acceptances from the members of each class to take up the full number of shares of each class offered by the transfer notice, the directors shall thereupon apportion shares so offered among the members so accepting and so far as may be, pro rata, according to the number of shares held by each of them respectively, and in the case of more than one class of shares, then pro rata in respect of each class. If the directors shall not have received sufficient acceptances as aforesaid, they may, but only with the consent of the proposing transferor who shall not be obliged to sell to members in the aggregate less than the total number of shares of one or more classes of shares offered by the transfer notice, apportion the shares so offered among the members so accepting so far as may be according to the number of shares held by each respectively but only up to the amount accepted by such members respectively. Upon any such apportionment being made the proposing transferor shall be bound upon payment of the price to transfer the shares to the respective members to whom the directors have apportioned same. If, in any case, the proposing transferor, having become so bound fails in transferring any share, the Company may receive the purchase money for that share and shall upon receipt cause the name of the purchasing member to be entered in the register as the holder of the shares and cancel the certificate of the share held by the proposed transferor, whether the same shall be produced to the Company or not, and shall hold such purchase money in trust for the proposing transferor. The receipt of the Company for the purchase money shall be a good discharge to the purchasing member and after his name has been entered in the register the validity of the proceedings shall not be questioned by any person.

(d)   In the event that some or all of the shares offered shall not be sold under the preceding Articles within the 14 day period referred to in Article 24.2 (b), the proposing transferor shall be at liberty for a period of 90 days after the expiration of that period to transfer such of the shares so offered as are not sold to any person provided that he shall not sell them at a price less than that specified in the transfer notice or on terms more favourable to a purchaser than those specified in the transfer notice.

(e)   The provisions as to transfer contained in this Article shall not apply:

(i)   if before the proposed transfer of shares is made, the transferor shall obtain consents to the proposed transfer from members of the Company, who at the time of the transfer are the registered holders of two-thirds or more of the issued shares of the class to be transferred of the Company or if the shares comprise more than one class, then from the registered holders of two-thirds or more of the shares of each class to be transferred and such consent shall be taken to be a waiver of the application of the preceding Articles as regards such transfer; or

(ii)   to a transfer of shares desired to be made merely for the purpose of effectuating the appointment of a new trustee for the owner thereof, provided that it is proved to the satisfaction of the Board that such is the case.

FULL NAME(S), ADDRESS(ES), AND OCCUPATION(S) OF SUBSCRIBERS

John Doe, Teacher
111 A Street
Anywhere, BC   Z1P 0G0

John Doe

Jack Doe, Businessman
222 B Street
Anywhere, BC   Z1P 0G0

Jack Doe

DATED at____Anywhere, BC_____, this_15th_ day of_____May_____, 20_0-__.

prohibit soliciting the public to buy shares. These restrictions are contained in Article 24 of the sample articles (see Sample 8). If you fail to include or comply with these provisions, the Securities Commission will consider your company to be a reporting company and prosecute and fine you for failing to comply with the provisions for reporting companies.

Understand that almost any restriction on share transfer will satisfy the Securities Commission. In the articles in Sample 8, the transfer is required to be approved by the directors — a common restriction for non-reporting companies. (However, if you prefer, you may require all transfers to be approved by the shareholders instead.)

Article 24 details the mechanics for obtaining the directors' approval to the share transfer. The selling shareholder must first offer his or her shares to the other shareholders before offering them to any strangers. To protect their percentage position in the company, the existing shareholders have the right to buy the shares on a "pro rata basis."

Pro rata means that the percentage of the shares up for sale that each shareholder may buy is determined by the proportion that each of the remaining shareholders' holdings bears in relation to all of the remaining shareholders' holders. For example, say Mary holds 100 shares in the Rimarri Cookie Company, Rick holds 60 shares, and Rita holds 40 shares. They are the only three shareholders. Mary decides to sell her shares. Since Rick holds 60% of the remaining shares, he could purchase 60% of Mary's shares, or 60 shares. Rita, whose 40 shares represent 40% of the remaining shares, could buy 40% of Mary's shares, or 40 shares.

No matter what restrictions on the transfer of shares you adopt, be sure to include them in your articles. Remember also

to type your company name on the fifth page under the heading "COMPANY ACT" ARTICLES OF. Have the people who signed the memorandum sign the articles in the same manner as they signed the bottom of the memorandum.

Note: On the articles you submit to the Registrar, do *not* fill in the sample proxy (found in Article 11.11 of Sample 8, or Article 9.8 of the Company Act's Table A articles).

6. DRAFT THE NOTICE OF REGISTERED AND RECORDS OFFICES

Another document you need to draft to incorporate your company is a Notice of Offices (see Sample 9). As with the memorandum and articles, you must prepare two copies of this document (available in the *Incorporation Forms and Disk for BC* kit).

The Company Act requires that all businesses incorporated within British Columbia have two offices within the province. They are a registered office, where legal documents may be served upon the company, and a records office, where registers and documents must be kept ready for inspection by shareholders, employees, creditors and the general public. Most companies have both offices at the same address. In many cases, this will be your primary place of business.

The locations of your registered and records offices must be places that can be found. The addresses may not be post office box numbers.

7. PROCEDURE FOR FILING DOCUMENTS

Whenever you file any documents, try to arrange for everyone to attend a single signing session, so all forms have the same date. Be sure all forms have the postal codes of all addresses listed.

SAMPLE 9
NOTICE OF OFFICES

BRITISH COLUMBIA

Ministry of Finance and Corporate Relations
Corporate and Personal Property Registries

Mailing Address:
PO Box 9431 Stn Prov Govt
Victoria BC V8W 9V3
Location:
2nd Floor – 940 Blanshard Street
Victoria BC

NOTICE OF OFFICES
Form 3
Section 8 *COMPANY ACT*

Telephone: (250) 356-8648
Hours: 8:30 – 4:30 (Monday – Friday)

A **FULL NAME OF COMPANY** – Please show the exact name as stated in the memorandum of the company

J & J Industries Ltd.

OFFICE USE ONLY – DO NOT WRITE IN THIS AREA

INSTRUCTIONS

1. **Please type or print clearly in block letters and ensure that the form is signed and dated in ink. Complete all areas of the form. The Registry may have to return documents that do not meet this standard.**

2. In Box B and C, enter the complete physical address of the office. You may include general delivery, post office box, rural route, site or comp. number as part of the address, but the Registry can not accept this information as a complete address. You must also include a postal code. If an area does not have street names or numbers, provide a description that would readily allow a person to locate the office.

Freedom of Information and Protection of Privacy Act
The personal information requested on this form is made available to the public under the authority of the *Company Act*. Questions about the collection or use of this information can be directed to the Administrative Analyst, Corporate and Personal Property Registries at (250) 356-0944, PO Box 9431 Stn Prov Govt, Victoria BC V8W 9V3.

B **REGISTERED OFFICE ADDRESS**

222A Street, Anywhere

PROVINCE	POSTAL CODE
BC	Z 1 P 0 G 0

C **RECORDS OFFICE ADDRESS**

333B Street, Anywhere

PROVINCE	POSTAL CODE
BC	Z 1 P 0 G 0

D **SIGNATURE OF SUBSCRIBER/SOLICITOR** – I have read this form and found it to be correct.

John Doe   SUBSCRIBER

DATE SIGNED
YYYY	MM	DD
2 0 0 -	0 5	1 5

FIN 720 Rev. 1999 / 3 / 10 (Prescribed)

To incorporate your company, you must submit two original copies of the following:

(a) Memorandum

(b) Articles

(c) Form 3 — the Notice of Offices

In the sample covering letter, shown in Sample 10, please note the reference to the Registrar's order number issued when you applied to reserve the company name. You should make a similar reference in your covering letter.

Submit the documents listed above, together with the cheque or money order covering the incorporation fees (made payable to the Minister of Finance), to the Registrar of Companies. You'll probably want to get back certified copies of your documents, so your payment will be $325 (basic incorporation fee plus fee for certified copies). Make sure you submit your documents within 56 calendar days of the date of approval of the company name.

While it isn't necessary to enclose these documents and your payment in a covering letter, a covering letter helps to ensure that the incorporation process goes smoothly. A sample covering letter is shown in Sample 10.

Applications for incorporation are processed on a first-come, first-served basis and usually take about two weeks. The Registrar offers a priority service on processing documents, so if you're in a hurry to receive your incorporation papers, you can pay a $100 fee on top of the regular incorporation fees and request priority service in your covering letter.

If your documents are in order, certified copies of the memorandum, articles, and Form 3 (Notice of Offices) will be returned to you along with the Certificate of Incorporation. These documents will normally be mailed to you, unless you tell the Corporate Registry in writing that you don't want them mailed. Your Certificate of Incorporation will resemble the one in Sample 11.

Remember that if your documents are rejected for any reason by the Registrar, you'll have to pay an additional fee when resubmitting your forms, so double-check all your forms for completeness of the required information and signatures before submitting them. You should also confirm by telephone the current fees, as fees given in this book may have changed since publication.

After your company has been incorporated, the Registrar will publish a notice of your incorporation in the *British Columbia Gazette* (see Sample 12).

SAMPLE 10
LETTER TO REGISTRAR

John Doe
123 East Street
Vancouver, BC
V1P 0G0

May 16, 200-

Registrar of Companies
Ministry of Finance and Corporate Relations
PO Box 9431
Victoria, BC
V8W 9V3

Re: Incorporation of
J & J Industries Ltd.

Enclosed are the following documents:

1. Two original signed copies of the Memorandum and Articles

2. Notice of Offices (Form 3 — two signed copies)

3. Our cheque in the amount of $325*, payable to the Minister of Finance, to cover your fees

The name J & J Industries Ltd. was reserved with your office under number 45678. Would you kindly attend to the incorporation of the above-mentioned company and return certified copies of the enclosed documents as soon as possible?

Thank you.

Yours truly,

John Doe
John Doe

*Note: This amount will vary depending on your circumstances and whether the fees have changed. Please check with the Registrar for current fees before submitting your documents.

SAMPLE 11
CERTIFICATE OF INCORPORATION

CANADA
PROVINCE OF BRITISH COLUMBIA

NUMBER

654321

Province of British Columbia

Ministry of Finance and Corporate Relations

REGISTRAR OF COMPANIES

Company Act

Certificate of Incorporation

I HEREBY CERTIFY THAT

J & J Industries Ltd.

HAS THIS DAY BEEN INCORPORATED UNDER THE COMPANY ACT

GIVEN UNDER MY HAND AND SEAL OF OFFICE

AT VICTORIA, BRITISH COLUMBIA,

THIS   1st   DAY OF   JUNE   , 200-

DEPUTY REGISTRAR OF COMPANIES

GAZETTE NOTICE
COMPANY ACT

The Registrar of Companies hereby gives notice of the incorporation of the following companies:

	January 15, 200-
654321	Sky-Glider Recreations (1986) Ltd.
	January 16, 200-
654654	Canwest Publishers Limited
	January 17, 200-
654823	Alderwood Projects Ltd.
654731	Alginure Products Canada Ltd.
654705	Amar Developments Ltd.

5
POST-INCORPORATION PROCEDURES

You've received your Certificate of Incorporation from Victoria. What do you do next?

1. PURCHASE MINUTE BOOK AND PREPARE REGISTERS

Under the Company Act, minutes of all company meetings must be kept at the records office. Therefore, if you haven't obtained a minute book, you should do so now. Insert the certified copies of the incorporation documents returned to you by the Registrar under the proper tabs in your minute book. (See the order form at the front of this book if you wish to obtain a minute book from the publisher.)

You must keep a director's register showing the full names and resident addresses of the directors and other specified information (see Sample 13, which shows all the information that must be kept). You must also keep shareholders' registers showing their full names and addresses and other specified information such as share allotments and share transfers. Samples 14, 15, and 16 show a sample shareholders' register, register of share allotments, and register of share transfers and the information required. (**Note:** The registers can be written; they don't need to be typed.)

Strictly speaking, you don't need a company seal. However, some banks prefer you "seal" all agreements that the company makes with the bank, and you may save yourself some trouble if you simply order a seal. If you decide to obtain a seal, you may order one from the publisher. However, don't order your seal until you

receive your Certificate of Incorporation from the Registrar. Any slight deviation from the company's name on the certificate will render the seal virtually useless.

2. MAINTAIN PROPER COMPANY RECORDS

In addition to the minutes and registers, the Company Act requires that certain other documents must also be physically kept at the company's records office (which is often the registered office too).

These provisions are to enable people like minority shareholders and creditors of the company to be well informed. They're also meant to encourage thorough record keeping by all British Columbia companies. There is little proof that this is the actual result of these requirements. But the penalties are severe, so it's imperative that you take steps to comply with the provisions regarding record keeping and inspection rights contained in the Company Act.

If it's a problem for you to keep your own records, you might consider using the "records office" services offered by many lawyers. The annual charge for this service usually ranges from $150 to $300.

2.1 What documents are kept at the records office?

The documents that must be kept at the records offices are listed in Table 2. The secretary of the company is responsible for filing and keeping these records (see chapter 13 for information on the duties and responsibilities of the company's officers).

Name of Company J & J Industries Ltd.

DIRECTORS

NAME	RESIDENT ADDRESS		Date Appointed or Elected	Date Ceased	OFFICE HELD		
					Office	Date Appointed	Date Ceased
John Doe	111 A Street Anywhere	BC	June 1/200-		President	June 29/200-	
Jack Doe	222 B Street Anywhere	BC	June 1/200-		Sec./Treas.	June 29/200-	

REGISTER OF
SHAREHOLDERS

Name of Company J & J Industries Ltd.   Page No. ___1

Date Became a Member	Date Ceased to be Member	Full Name and Address	Representative Capacity	Class & Kind of Share	Par Value	Acquired by Allotments Conversion Transfer (or)	If Transferred From Whom	Cert. No.	Consideration Paid to Company			
									Agreed Per Share	Paid Per Share		
										Cash	Other than Cash	
											Amount	Particulars
June 1 200–		John Doe 111 A Street Anywhere, BC Z1P 0G0	50	Comm.	NPV	Allot.		1	$0.01	$0.01		
June 1 200–		Jack Doe 222 B Street Anywhere, BC Z1P 0G0	50	Comm.	NPV	Allot.		2	$0.01	$0.01		

REGISTER OF SHARE ALLOTMENTS

REGISTER OF
ALLOTMENTS

Name of Company J & J Industries Ltd.   Page No. ___1___

Date of Allotment	To Whom Alloted — Name and Address	Shares Alloted — Quantity	Class and Kind	Par Value	Certificate Issued No.	Consideration — Cash or Other Considerations	Amount Paid on Each Share	No. of Shares Allowed for Cash	No. of Shares Alloted for Other Considerations Particulars of Contract	Commission or Discount per Share Allowed or Agreed to be Allowed
June 1 200-	John Doe 111 A Street Anywhere, BC Z1P 0G0	50	Comm.	NPV	1	$0.50	$0.01	50		
June 1 200-	Jack Doe 222 B Street Anywhere, BC Z1P 0G0	50	Comm.	NPV	2	$0.50	$0.01	50		
Aug. 3 200-	John Doe	100	Comm.	NPV	3	$50.00	$0.50	100		
Aug. 3 200-	Jack Doe	100	Comm.	NPV	4	$50.00	$0.50	100		

68

SAMPLE 16
REGISTER OF SHARE TRANSFERS

REGISTER OF TRANSFERS

Name of Company J & J Industries Ltd.

Page No. 1

Date			Certificate Surrendered			Name of Transferor	Name of Transferee	Certificate Issued		
			Kind & Class	Cert. Number	Shares			Kind & Class	Cert. Number	Shares
Aug.	3	200–	Comm.	4	100	John Doe	Jean Doe	Comm.	7	50
Aug.	3	200–	Comm.	5	100	Jack Doe	Jean Doe	Comm.	7	50

69

TABLE 2
DOCUMENTS REQUIRED TO BE KEPT AT RECORDS OFFICE

Records office documents

163.   (1) Records office documents — Every company shall keep at its records office

   (a)   its certificate of incorporation,

   (b)   a copy of its memorandum, including every amendment of it,

   (c)   a copy of its articles, including every amendment of them,

   (d)   its register of members, except as provided by section 69,

   (e)   its register of transfers, unless the register of members is kept elsewhere as provided by section 69,

   (f)   its register of directors,

   (g)   its register of debentureholders, except as provided by section 78 or 79,

   (h)   its register of debentures,

   (i)   its register of indebtedness,

   (j)   its register of allotments, unless the register of members is kept elsewhere as provided by section 69,

   (k)   the minutes of every general meeting and class meeting of the company,

   (l)   the minutes of every meeting of its directors,

   (m)   a copy of every document filed with the registrar,

   (n)   a copy of every certificate issued to it by the registrar,

   (o)   a copy of every order of the minister or the registrar relating to the company,

   (p)   a copy of every written contract under which the company has allotted any shares for a consideration other than cash,

   (q)   a copy of every other document and instrument approved in the preceding 10 years by the directors,

   (r)   a copy of every mortgage created or assumed by the company, whether or not required to be registered,

   (s)   a copy of every audited financial statement of the company and its subsidiaries, whether or not consolidated with the financial statement of the company, including the auditor's reports,

   (t)   where the company is an amalgamated company,

      (i)   every record, document, or instrument described in paragraphs (a) to (j), (m) to (p), and (u) to (w);

      (ii)   every record, document, or instrument described in paragraphs (l), (q), and (r); and

      (iii)   every record, document, or instrument described in paragraphs (k) and (s); of each of the amalgamating companies,

TABLE 2 — Continued

(u) if the company is being wound up, the minutes of every meeting of its creditors,

(v) a copy of every prospectus and takeover bid circular issued in the preceding 10 years by the company or any subsidiary;

(w) a copy of every information circular issued in the preceding 10 years by the company or any subsidiary,

(x) a copy of the instrument of continuation under section 36, if any, and

(y) if a receiver or receiver-manager is appointed under an instrument registered in the office of the registrar, the name and address of the receiver or receiver-manager, the date of the appointment of the receiver or receiver-manager, and the date the receiver or receiver-manager ceases to act or complete the duties of that office.

(2) Except as provided in subsection (3), the records, documents, and instruments referred to in subsection (1) are those established or made, and the information in them relates to matters occurring after October 1, 1973.

(3) The records, documents, and instruments referred to in subsection (1)(a) to (d), (g), and (k) are those relating to matters occurring since the incorporation of the company, or of the amalgamating companies, as the case may be, but, with respect to the period before October 1, 1973, only to the extent that the records, documents, or instruments referred to in those paragraphs were required to be kept by the provisions of any former Companies Act.

(4) Every company that contravenes this section commits an offence.

2.2 Who may see the records?

A person's rights to review the company records depends on his or her relationship to the company (i.e., shareholder, creditor).

For example, every director may examine and take copies of all the documents listed in section 163 of the Company Act (see Table 2) at no charge. A former director has the same privileges concerning the examination of documents that relate to the time of his or her directorship.

Every shareholder is entitled to a free copy of the memorandum and articles. In addition, if you're a shareholder or debenture holder (i.e., loaned money to the company secured by a debenture), you may look at and copy any document listed in Table 2 for free, except for items in paragraphs (l), (q), (r), and (t)(ii).

For a fee of 50¢ for each document looked at (or less, if prescribed by the company), anyone may look at and copy any document except those in paragraphs (k), (l),(q), (r), (s), and (t)(ii) and (iii) of section 163 of the Company Act (see Table 2).

Your records office must be set up so that the listed documents and registers are available for inspection for at least two consecutive normal business hours per business day.

You may keep the company records in bound or loose-leaf form or by electrical or mechanical data processing. But whatever form you choose, you must be able to reproduce the required information within a reasonable time. Your records office must be set up so that the documents can be promptly accessed.

You must also see that the documents are reasonably protected from loss or destruction and from being falsified. This means that someone must be there whenever anyone looks at the company records to ensure that no alterations or false entries are made.

Your records office will also likely be responsible for responding to any requests for a list of shareholders or debenture holders. If an applicant makes a request in writing, the company must prepare a list with the shareholders' names and addresses and the number of shares each holds, or the names and addresses of all debenture holders. This list must be current to within 14 days of delivering the list, and the company may charge a reasonable fee for preparing the list.

The applicant must include an affidavit in his or her written request, disclosing the name of the applicant and promising that the list will only be used for "corporate purposes." This means that the list will be used in an effort to solicit votes of shareholders or debenture holders at a meeting to acquire or sell shares or debentures, to cause the company to amalgamate, or to make some other reorganization.

If you don't keep the required records or refuse to let a shareholder examine them, you are guilty of an offence and liable to a serious fine. If you authorize or permit any of these offences as a director, you're also guilty of an offence and personally liable for any fines. If you're responsible for the accuracy of the company records, and if a false statement is made in any record, or if an important material fact is left out, then you may be found guilty of an offence and liable to a fine. Company secretaries take note!

3.   BANKING ARRANGEMENTS

Your company, since it is a separate legal entity, must have its own bank account

and deposit, withdrawal, and chequing arrangements. These arrangements are determined by resolutions of the company and by agreement with the bank.

You may wish to consider opening an account at a trust company or credit union. Unlike banks, trust companies and credit unions normally pay interest on chequing accounts. However, if you need financing, a bank is probably your best bet because it will lend money on security, like an assignment of accounts receivable, whereas a trust company or credit union advances loans mainly on mortgages, and will not accept other types of security.

Your bank manager will provide the necessary forms (banking resolutions) for you to fill out.

4.   POST-INCORPORATION ORGANIZATION

After you've bought your minute book and decided what bank your company is going to use, you must prepare the consent resolutions that organize the company's affairs.

Although these resolutions don't have to be filed with the Registrar of Companies, it is very important to have them signed and kept in the minute book. That way, if at a later date, a dissident shareholder or director challenges certain company proceedings, the documents are on file for ready inspection. This happens more often than you may think, and you leave yourself open for trouble if these resolutions aren't prepared and then signed by all parties concerned.

4.1   Subscribers' resolutions

Your first resolution will be by the subscribers to the memorandum. You want a resolution that formally approves and adopts the documents of incorporation, elects the directors, and waives the necessity for having an audit for the first year.

To simplify matters, the resolutions in Sample 17 combine the resolutions of the first directors and the subscribers to the memorandum, as is done in many law firms. In this sample, the first few resolutions, down to "Election of Officers," are the subscribers' section. By reading them, you'll understand what you're supposed to do.

4.2 Directors' resolutions

Next comes the preparation of the directors' section. As you can see from Sample 17, the first resolutions of the directors are usually designed to transfer the subscribers' shares to permanent shareholders (if applicable), elect officers, appoint a banker, authorize transfer of assets into the company (again, if applicable), and other miscellaneous transactions.

Remember, it is the directors who sit in power and who, theoretically, direct the company on all important issues. Whenever an important issue arises, it is resolved by the directors and confirmed by a resolution in writing as shown in Sample 17.

4.3 Consents to act as director

Every director must consent in writing to act as a director unless present at the meeting at which he or she is elected (see Sample 28.) As most closely held companies pass consent resolutions, a consent to act as director should be signed by every director.

5. USE OF THE COMPANY NAME

In British Columbia, all companies must display their names legibly on the outside of all places of business, on contracts, business letters, orders for goods, invoices, statements, receipts, and letters of credit. Promissory notes, bills of exchange, cheques, and money orders must also receive the same treatment if they're made on behalf of the company (see section 106 of the Company Act).

Further, an officer who misleads someone by authorizing or issuing a document that doesn't properly display the company name is personally responsible for making good any loss arising from misleading the recipient.

Only companies are permitted to use the words "limited," "limited liability," "incorporated," "corporation," "non-personal liability," or the abbreviations of these words. Those who don't follow this section are liable to a fine of $50 per day for each day that business is done under the improper name (section 107).

You should note especially section 107 (4), which makes officers and directors personally responsible for indemnifying any persons who suffer a loss or damage as a result of being misled by the officer's or director's failure to insist the company name be displayed on a document such as a cheque or promissory note.

73

SAMPLE 17
CONSENT RESOLUTIONS OF SUBSCRIBER AND FIRST DIRECTORS

<u>_____J & J Industries Ltd._____</u>
(the "Company")

We, the undersigned, being all the subscribers to the Memorandum and the first directors of the Company, consent in writing to the following resolutions:

CERTIFICATE OF INCORPORATION

The Company was incorporated on the <u>1st</u> day of <u>June</u>, 200 – <u>____</u> under incorporation number <u>654321</u>.

COMPANY SEAL

RESOLVED that the Company seal, an impression of which is shown in the margin of these resolutions, be adopted as the common seal of the Company.

ALLOTMENT OF SHARES

RESOLVED that the following shares be allotted and issued to the subscribers at the price of <u>$0.01</u> each as fully paid and non-assessable:

Cert. No.	Subscriber's Name	No. and Class of Shares
1	John Doe	50 Common shares without par value
2	Jack Doe	50 Common shares without par value

and that their names and other particulars in respect of such shares, be entered in the registers of allotments and members.

NUMBER OF DIRECTORS

RESOLVED that the number of directors of the Company be determined at <u>   two (2)   </u>

APPOINTMENT OF DIRECTORS

RESOLVED that the following persons, having consented in writing, be appointed the first directors of the Company:

    John Doe
    Jack Doe

AUDITOR

RESOLVED that the appointment of an auditor be waived pursuant to Section 179 of the Company Act until the first annual general meeting of the Company.

or

RESOLVED that_____ of _____
be appointed to act as auditor for the Company at a remuneration to be fixed by the directors of the Company.

ELECTION OF OFFICERS

RESOLVED that the following persons be appointed to the offices set opposite their respective names:

```
President:   John Doe

Secretary/Treasurer:  Jack Doe
```

QUORUM OF DIRECTORS

RESOLVED that the quorum for meetings of directors be fixed at_____2_____.

BANKERS

RESOLVED that the directors opens and maintains a bank acount in the name of the Company at Anywhere
 Credit Union, Main Branch, 200 Granville Avenue, Vancouver, BC
and that the resolution as to signing officers be annexed to these resolutions.

SHAREHOLDERS' LOANS

RESOLVED that the Company borrow the sum of one thousand dollars ($1 000)
from each of the member/directors and that the said shareholders' loans be secured by Demand Notes

RESOLVED that the Company execute the said Demand Notes in such manner as to give
full effect to the transactions hereinbefore described.

ACCOUNTING RECORDS

```
RESOLVED that the accounting records of the Company be kept at the Company's
head office or principal place of business or at such other place as the
director may from time to time determine.
```

INSPECTION TIMES

```
RESOLVED that, pursuant to section 164(5) of the Company Act, the examination
of the records of the Company by any person other than the directors of the
Company shall be restricted to two consecutive hours daily during normal
business hours, namely, from 10:00 a.m. to 12:00 noon each day.
```

TRANSFER OF ASSETS

RESOLVED that the Company purchase equipment as follows:

1. 1998 Chevrolet, Serial #123456JD89 from member/director John Doe $14 800.00.
2. 1989 Pontiac, Serial #98765SD12 from member/director Jack Doe $1 800.00.
3. Miscellaneous equipment and supplies from the members/directors jointly $500.00.

and that the said purchases shall be secured by Demand Notes.

RESOLVED that the Company execute the said_____Demand Notes_____ in such manner as required to give full effect to the transactions hereinbefore described.

YEAR END

RESOLVED that the financial year end of the Company be_____December 31st_____ of each year.

The foregoing resolutions are consented to in writing by the subscribers to the Memorandum and the first directors of the Company.

Dated as of the 29th day of June, 200-

John Doe
John Doe

Jack Doe
Jack Doe

6
COMPLYING WITH GOVERNMENT REGULATIONS

Certain government licences and regulations affect you and your business. This chapter contains a summary of the things you need to know to keep you and your business in good standing with the government. You may also want to read two very good guides available on the Internet:

(a) *Solutions for Small Business (Resource Guide for BC Businesses),* published by the BC Ministry of Small Business, Tourism, and Culture and Western Economic Development Canada. See <www.sb.gov.bc/smallbus/lotus/sbguides2.htm>.

(b) *Guide for Canadian Small Businesses,* published by the Canada Customs and Revenue Agency (formerly Revenue Canada). See <www.ccra-adrc.gc.ca/E/pub/tg/rc4070ed/rc4070ed.html>.

Note: Revenue Canada is now called the Canada Customs and Revenue Agency. CCRA is used throughout this chapter to refer to what used to be known as Revenue Canada.

1. KEEPING ACCOUNTS

Your company's books and records will be audited by federal and provincial agencies from time to time. Therefore, you might as well establish from the beginning an orderly records and accounts system which will be readily accessible.

To do this, you'll need the help of a good accountant. The best way to find someone is to ask your successful business friends — people you admire in a business

sense — to supply you with names. Then talk to at least three of them before making a choice.

If you want to learn something about accounting before you talk to an accountant so you can ask some intelligent questions, please refer to *Basic Accounting for the Small Business,* another title in the Self-Counsel Series, for a simplified explanation of the accounting process.

You can expect to have your books examined by the following government departments:

- Workers' Compensation Board

- CCRA — Taxation (which will include auditing of the goods and services tax (GST) as well as payroll auditing of employment insurance premiums, Canada Pension Plan contributions, and income tax deductions at source)

- CCRA — Customs and Excise

The provincial department of finance administers the social services tax and will also audit your books for this.

You must keep your books and records, including supporting documents — such as sales and purchase invoices, contracts, bank statements, and cancelled cheques — in an orderly manner at your place of business or designated records office.

The taxation branch of the Canada Customs and Revenue Agency requires that you keep all business records and supporting documents for six years. For income tax, the six-year period runs from the end of the last taxation year to which the records relate. For GST, the six-year period runs from the end of the year to which the records relate. If you wish to destroy your business books or records before the six years are up, you must apply in writing to the director of the district taxation office. You must also provide detailed information identifying the material and the fiscal period covered by such books.

Note: Some records must be kept indefinitely. These include the minute book, share records, general and private ledger sheets, special contracts and agreements, and the general journal if it is essential to the understanding of the general ledger entries.

2. FEDERAL REQUIREMENTS AND REGULATIONS

2.1 Goods and services tax

The goods and services tax (GST) is a value-added tax imposed by the federal government. Under the GST, a business collects tax from its customers. The tax is calculated as the sale price of taxable goods or services multiplied by 7%.

A business is entitled to claim a credit for any GST paid on the purchase of goods or services used in its business. This credit (an input tax credit) is available to each business in the production and distribution chain. The final non-business consumer of the good or service doesn't get a tax credit for the GST he or she pays. The final non-business consumer therefore bears the burden of the tax.

The total amount of GST collected in a given period, less the input tax credits for that period, must be remitted to the Canada Customs and Revenue Agency. If, in any given period, the input tax credits exceed the tax collected, a business will be entitled to a refund equal to the difference.

In general, all goods and services sold, leased, or transferred in Canada are subject to GST. However, certain specified goods and services (such as basic groceries and health care) aren't taxable.

All businesses with gross sales in the preceding year that exceed $30 000 are required to register with the CCRA for purposes of collecting and remitting GST on their sales. See section **2.7** later in this chapter for more information on how to register.

A business with gross sales below $30 000 is known as a small supplier, and registration is optional. Unregistered businesses don't have to charge GST on their sales, but they can't recover GST paid on their purchases. Therefore, even if your sales are under $30 000, you might want to register your corporation so you can claim a credit for the GST your company pays.

In order to claim the input tax credit, your corporation must keep detailed records of all GST it has paid. There is an escape from this if you use the so-called "quick method" of GST accounting. (Use of the quick method is limited to businesses with annual sales of $200 000 or less.) Under this method, you still collect the full 7% GST on your sales, but you don't remit all of this to the government — instead you only send a portion. You cannot then claim the input tax credit or expenses, though you can still claim the credit on capital items.

2.2 Federal excise tax

An excise tax is imposed on certain specific goods manufactured or produced in Canada or imported into Canada. The list of excisable items includes jewellery, matches, cigarettes, and tobacco. Complete details can be found in the Excise Tax Act. To obtain a copy of the act, check in your local library, or you may buy a copy from Canadian Clearing House (CCH) by calling 1-800-461-5308.

The Canada Customs and Revenue Agency requires that all persons or firms manufacturing or producing goods subject to an excise tax operate under a manufacturer's excise tax licence ("E" licence). You can obtain this licence from the regional or district excise tax office of the CCRA in the area in which you or your company propose to operate.

However, you don't need an E licence if you're a small manufacturer. You qualify as a small manufacturer if your total annual sales don't exceed $50 000. You may also buy goods for resale without paying excise taxes if you have a wholesaler licence ("W" licence). If you qualify for a W licence, you collect and pay the excise tax at the time you sell the goods. In addition, in certain circumstances, you may be able to claim a refund of excise taxes paid.

For more information about excise taxes, contact:

Canada Customs and
  Revenue Agency, Taxation
Vancouver Tax Services Office
1166 West Pender Street
Vancouver, BC V6E 3H8
Telephone: (604) 689-5411 or
  1-800-959-5525

2.3   Customs duties

Any business that imports products from abroad must be aware of customs duties that are levied against goods upon entry into Canada. There are regulations concerning invoicing, classification of goods, rates of duty, and reductions, and exemptions for special classes of articles.

If you're planning to import goods into Canada, you should obtain a ruling on the classification, rate of duty, and valuation before commencing shipments. For more information, contact:

Canada Customs and Revenue
  Agency, Customs and Excise
Main Floor, 333 Dunsmuir Street
Vancouver, BC V6B 5R4
Telephone: (604) 666-0545 or
  1-800-461-9999

2.4   Federal income tax

The federal government levies both personal and corporate income tax on monies earned in Canada. Income taxes are applied on income received or receivable during the taxation year from all sources inside and outside Canada, less certain deductions. Individuals and branches of foreign companies carrying on business in Canada are also liable for income taxes on profits earned from these business operations. Small businesses qualify for special tax rates. See chapter 2 for further information on corporate income tax and tax tips for small businesses.

If you are an employer, you must deduct personal income tax from the pay cheques of all employees on a regular basis. Most employers must remit their deductions before the 15th day of the month after the month that the deduction was made. But small-business employers may be able to remit deductions once every three months.

You may make your payments at any Canadian financial institution. You must start to deduct employee benefits when the employee begins to work for you.

Companies have to pay their corporate income tax in regular monthly installments. The balance of the tax owing by your company must usually be paid within two months of the end of that taxation year (three months in certain circumstances). You can mail your company's cheque to the Receiver General at the Surrey Tax Centre address listed below or pay the tax owing directly at a Canadian financial institution.

Every company has to file an income tax return ("T2" return) for each taxation year, even if there is no tax payable. When filing your company's return, send complete financial statements and all necessary schedules. The T2 return must be filed within six months of the company's fiscal year end.

For specific information about federal income tax and deductions, contact the Canada Customs and Revenue Agency, Taxation at:

Tax Centre
Surrey, BC V3T 5E1
Telephone: 1-888-738-7718

or

Canada Customs and Revenue
  Agency, Taxation
Vancouver Tax Services Office
1166 West Pender Street
Vancouver, BC V6E 3H8
Telephone: (604) 689-5411 or
  1-800-959-5525

2.5   Employment insurance

In Canada, workers who become unemployed may qualify for employment insurance (EI) benefits (previously called unemployment insurance or UI) under a federal government program.

With few exceptions, all employment in Canada performed under a contract of service is insurable, and, therefore, subject to employment insurance premium payments by both the employer and the employee.

The employer must collect employees' premiums according to current premium scales. Deductions may be paid at any Canadian financial institution.

All matters relating to deductions, remittances, and rulings for employment insurance premiums are handled by the Canada Customs and Revenue Agency, Taxation. For more information, contact:

Canada Customs and
  Revenue Agency, Taxation
Vancouver Tax Services Office
1166 West Pender Street
Vancouver, BC V6E 3H8
Telephone: (604) 689-5411 or
  1-800-959-5525

2.6   Canada Pension Plan

The Canada Pension Plan (CPP) is designed to provide a basic retirement pension for working Canadians. Employees between the ages of 18 and 70 in most types of employment are covered by the plan and must contribute.

Types of non-pensionable employment include agriculture, horticulture, fishing, hunting, forestry, logging, or lumbering, where the employee earns less than $2 500 in cash per year.

The employer is responsible for making the deductions from salaries of eligible employees. In addition, the employer must match these deductions with similar contributions. A person who is self-employed is responsible for the entire annual contribution to the Canada Pension Plan. The deductions may be paid at any Canadian financial institution.

Note: If you are incorporated and pay yourself a wage, as far as the Canada Pension Plan is concerned, you're not self-employed. You should deduct the normal amount from your wage, and the company must also contribute as the employer.

For more information about deducting and paying CPP premiums, contact:

Canada Customs and Revenue
  Agency, Taxation
Vancouver Tax Services Office
1166 West Pender Street
Vancouver, BC V6E 3H8
Telephone: (604) 689-5411 or
  1-800-959-5525

2.7 Business Number

You'll need a federal Business Number (BN) if you have or need at least one of the following four business accounts with the Canada Customs and Revenue Agency:

- Corporate income tax

- Import/export (excise tax and customs duties)

- Payroll deductions (employees' income tax, employment insurance, and Canada Pension Plan)

- GST

Your BN has 15 digits and is made up of two parts — the registration number and the account identifier. The registration number consists of the first nine digits, which identify your business. The account identifier consists of two letters, which identify the account (corporate income tax, import/export, payroll deductions, or GST), and the last four digits, which identify the number of that account (e.g., a second or third payroll deductions account).

You can register for your BN by telephone, in person, by mail or fax, or at an OSBR computer workstation. To obtain an application form, contact the CCRA at 1-800-959-2221 (toll free), download an application form from the Canada Customs and Revenue Agency's Web site at <www.ccra-adrc.gc.ca>, or visit an OSBR centre. You'll have to send a copy of your company's certificate of incorporation to the CCRA by mail or fax to complete your registration. The address is:

Canada Customs and Revenue
  Agency, Taxation
Vancouver Tax Services Office
1166 West Pender Street
Vancouver, BC V6E 3H8
Fax: (604) 691-3995

To register, you'll need to have certain basic information at hand, including the following:

- The name and social insurance number of an officer or director

- The certificate of incorporation number

- The date of incorporation

- An estimate of your business' sales and revenues

If your company is an employer, the CCRA can help you calculate the amount of employment insurance, Canada Pension Plan, and income tax deductions to be made from your employees' salaries when you apply for your business number.

Shortly after registering, you'll receive a letter from the CCRA confirming your BN and the accounts you have opened.

3. PROVINCIAL GOVERNMENT REQUIREMENTS AND REGULATIONS

3.1 Licensing

There are certain specific provincial acts containing licensing regulations and requirements that apply to specific businesses. It's impossible to list all the provincial acts and the businesses to which they apply. But the following is a list of some of the more common businesses that fall under provincial administration, and you should be concerned if you operate a business in any of these areas:

- Door-to-door sales, pyramid schemes, or franchises

- Lending money or involved in any way with the consumer finance business

- Manufacturing (especially regarding labour laws and factory standards)

- Handling or processing food

- Transportation (goods or persons)

- Child care and adult care-giving services

- Dealing with natural resources, such as forests, minerals, or water

- Fish processing

- Pollution standards (including pesticides)

- Carrying on a business on provincially owned land, such as parks and beaches

For more information, contact the provincial ministry in charge of the business activity your company will be engaged in to ensure your business is properly licensed and following current regulations.

3.2 The Workers' Compensation Board (WCB)

The Workers' Compensation Board (WCB) provides rehabilitation services and financial and medical assistance to workers who are injured on the job. The Workers' Compensation Act is meant to provide a way for the worker to receive assistance without having to go to court first to sue his or her employer or fellow employees. In most cases, people are entitled to benefits under the act, regardless of who was at fault in causing the injury. Compensation costs are funded by assessments paid by employers.

All incorporated businesses must register with the Workers' Compensation Board. All shareholders and officers involved in the company's business — even if only to a small degree — are considered employees.

Note: If you operate your business through a limited company, you're not self-employed as far as the Workers' Compensation Board (WCB) is concerned. Your company is the employer; you are an employee.

If you hire people classified as independent operators who work on a consulting or "freelance" basis, these people won't be considered your employees, and you may not be responsible for making the payroll assessments to the board for their wages. The kind of worker who can be classified as an independent operator varies depending on the business or industry. You should check with the WCB (see below) about anyone who does any work for you. Sometimes, even a casual labourer hired for just a few hours may have to be covered.

A pamphlet and application form will normally be mailed to the registered office of each company shortly after incorporation. You can register with the WCB by telephone or fax or by mailing in your application to:

Workers' Compensation Board
  Assessment Department
PO Box 5350 Stn. Terminal
Vancouver, BC V6B 5L5
Fax: (604) 244-6490
Telephone: (604) 244-6182 or
  1-888-922-2768

When you register, you'll be sent a confirmation letter containing your registration number, your payroll assessment rates for that year, and your remittance cycle (when the rates will be sent to you and when you have to send in your payments). You'll also receive a sample claim form and information on basic occupational safety and health, accident prevention, and working with the WCB.

The amount you have to pay depends on two things: the accident-prone "rating" of the industry you're in and the total payroll of your company. Even if you, as the principal shareholder, draw little or no salary, you may be "assessed" a higher salary level for purposes of WCB coverage.

WCB assessments must be paid totally by the employer (i.e., the company). You cannot deduct a portion from the employee's wages.

What happens if you fail to register with the board? For one thing, you're guilty of committing an offence and, if an employee is injured and his or her claim is allowed, your company will have to bear the total compensation costs of the claim. All unpaid assessments will have to be made up as well. If you are the principal of an unregistered company, you won't receive compensation for your injuries and you may be liable for a penalty.

Unpaid assessments constitute an unregistered lien on all real estate and on machinery or other goods owned by the company. They actually rank in priority over registered mortgages and other charges (like a mechanic's lien). The delinquent assessment fees may be recovered from your company when the asset is sold, or from any subsequent purchaser.

If you need assistance or any additional information, be sure to contact your nearest WCB office, or call the WCB's Employer Service Centre at the number listed above. Also check the WCB Web site at <www.worksafebc.com>.

3.3 Sales tax

The British Columbia government imposes a sales or social services tax (known as provincial sales tax or PST). At present, the tax on most goods and services is 7%. Most businesses must collect this tax from their customers or consumers and remit it to the government.

You're required to register as a vendor under the Social Service Tax Act if you regularly sell or lease tangible personal property on a retail basis. For example, if you regularly sell or lease any of the following, you must collect and remit PST:

- Alcoholic beverages

- Building materials
- Motor vehicles or automotive parts and supplies
- Flowers
- Cigarettes
- Propane
- Household or office furniture
- General goods such as clothing, art supplies, cosmetics, and appliances

You must also be registered if you sell a taxable service. Examples of taxable services include:

- Watch repairs and maintenance
- Automobile service and repairs
- Furniture repairs and refinishing
- Installation of computer software
- Maintenance of business equipment such as photocopiers, computers, and cash registers

To register as a vendor, you must complete an application form available from all Consumer Taxation Branch offices. The main office is located in Victoria at:

Consumer Taxation Branch
1061 Fort Street
PO Box 9442, Stn. Prov. Govt.
Victoria, BC V8W 9V4
Telephone: (250) 387-0656
Fax: (250) 387-6218

Upon application, a registration certificate assigning a tax number will be issued to you by the provincial consumer taxation branch.

As a registered vendor, this certificate exempts you from paying tax on merchandise or services you purchase for resale purposes. Simply quote your registration number to your suppliers.

4. MUNICIPAL GOVERNMENT REQUIREMENTS AND REGULATIONS

4.1 Licensing

The Municipal Act authorizes every municipality to license businesses within its boundaries. Incorporated centres issue licences and permits based on local bylaws. Licence fees depend on the type of business operated. Communities can control aspects of zoning, land use, construction, and renovation for all types of business activities including the licensing of commercial vehicles.

Contact your local city hall or municipal office for information in these areas. In unincorporated areas, contact the nearest government agent or RCMP detachment.

4.2 Municipal taxes

Municipal governments levy taxes on real estate, water consumption, and business premises.

Property taxes are based on the assessed real value of the land and improvements. Annual notices of assessment are sent out with provision for appeal.

Local business taxes are applied directly against the tenant or the business operator. The business tax may be a flat rate based on the number of employees you have or it may be assessed on a percentage of the annual rental value. These taxes may be incorporated into the annual business licence fee you must pay.

4.3 Building requirements

All three levels of government have some responsibility for regulating commercial building. Any construction which is proposed must satisfy all the requirements of the three governments.

The city hall or municipal office brings together all the various building codes and inspections, making it possible for approval of planned construction to be obtained at the local level.

The municipality controls the type of building you may construct. Municipal building and zoning regulations control the physical structure and the final use of your building. The municipality also has the power to enforce building regulations.

Before beginning construction or renovation of a structure, you must obtain a building permit from the municipality. To apply, you must submit preliminary sketches for approval and, when the sketches have received approval, submit complete construction drawings which will be examined to ensure that they meet the federal, provincial, and municipal building standards. If approval is given, you'll be issued a building permit.

Once construction has been started, various stages of the construction must be inspected before the project can continue.

As each municipality controls certain aspects of construction, the requirements vary from one area to another, so you should contact the building department of your municipal government office for specific requirements.

5. MISCELLANEOUS MATTERS

5.1 The metric system

The Canadian government has established a policy of promoting the use of metric measurements throughout the country. Compliance is mandatory in some areas of business. For further information on how you should be using the metric system in your business, check the Web site of Industry Canada, Measurement Canada: <mc.ic.gc.ca>. You can also contact them at:

Industry Canada, Measurement Canada
3625 Lougheed Highway
Vancouver, BC V5M 2A6
Telephone: (604) 666-3834

5.2 Weights and measures

Industry Canada, Measurement Canada is also responsible for the approval and inspection of all weighing and measuring devices, such as scales and fuel dispensers, that are used in trade.

Only approved measuring instruments can be used in business in Canada. Measurement Canada must inspect all new trade devices before first use. If you acquire used weighing equipment for commercial use, you should notify Measurement Canada. Those devices requiring installation before being inspected (e.g., vehicle scales), must be inspected on site when operational. Movable devices may be factory inspected before shipping, and Measurement Canada must be notified when this equipment is in place. It is necessary to report any relocation of the equipment to the department to ensure that regular inspections can continue to take place.

The period between inspections varies but is usually every two years. You are responsible for the cost of the initial inspections.

For further information or to arrange for an inspection, contact the nearest Measurement Canada office of Industry Canada, or you may contact:

> Industry Canada, Measurement
>   Canada
> 3625 Lougheed Highway
> Burnaby, BC V5M 2A6
> Telephone: (604) 666-3834

5.3 Packaging and labelling

Any prepackaged consumer product, including food and inedible items, is subject to the packaging regulations set out in the federal Consumer Packaging and Labelling Act.

Prepackaged products require a label stating the product's net quantity. The information must be declared in metric units and, optionally, in Imperial units of measure, and must appear in French and English. The identity of the product must also be given in both French and English.

There are also restrictions on the permissible size of the packages and for certain products only specific sizes are allowed.

In some instances, other information may be required. For example, hazardous or dangerous products must be properly marked, according to the Hazardous Products Act.

Textiles must be labelled with the fibre content according to the Textile Labelling Act. This act provides for the mandatory labelling of such textile articles as wearing apparel, fabrics sold by the piece, and household textiles. It also regulates the advertising, sale, and importation of all consumer textile fabric products.

Articles such as jewellery, silverware, optical products, watches, pens, and pencils, which are made wholly or partly of precious metals, are regulated by the Precious Metals Marking Act. Quality marks that are applied to the article must accurately show the quality of the precious metal, for example, 18kt.

For detailed information concerning the packaging and labelling of textiles and jewellery, check the Web site of the Competition Bureau of Industry Canada at <competition.ic.gc.ca>. You can call the Bureau's Information Centre at 1-800-348-5358. In British Columbia, you may contact the Competition Bureau at:

> Fair Business Practices Branch
> Industry Canada, Competition Bureau
> Suite 2000, 300 West Georgia Street
> Vancouver, BC V6B 6E1
> Telephone: (604) 666-5000

The Canadian Food Inspection Agency is responsible for the regulations concerning food. You may contact them at:

Canadian Food Inspection Agency
Room 103, 620 Royal Avenue
New Westminster, BC V3M 1J2
Telephone: (604) 666-6038

5.4   Intellectual property

Patents, copyrights, trademarks, industrial designs, and integrated circuit topographies are collectively called intellectual property. The laws concerning intellectual property are very complicated, and professional help is useful. Registered patent and trademark lawyers specialize in these fields, and consultation with them will ensure you get the best help.

For more information on patents, copyrights, trademarks, industrial designs, and integrated circuit topographies, check the Web site of the Canadian Intellectual Property office at <cipo.gc.ca>. Inquiries should be directed to:

Canadian Intellectual Property Office
Place du Portage Phase 1
50 Victoria Street
Hull, QC K1A 0C9
Telephone: (819) 997-1936

Note: Even though you may register your rights to ownership of the intellectual property described below, *enforcement* is your responsibility; the Canadian Intellectual Property office doesn't help with enforcing your rights. Registration provides you with proof of your rights. If you want to stop someone who has copied your invention or infringed on your rights, you'll have to enforce your rights through the courts.

5.4.a   Patents

Patents are used to protect inventions. A patent is a contract between the federal government and an inventor to exclude others from using the invention in Canada. The invention can be a product, a composition of materials, an apparatus or machine, or a process or method for making something.

Patents are granted for inventions that are new and useful and show some inventive ingenuity. The term of a patent is 20 years from the date of filing, and yearly fees are required to keep the patent alive.

If you wish to apply for a patent, you must submit a patent application with the appropriate fee to the Commissioner of Patents at the Canadian Intellectual Property office (see address above). The application must meet all the requirements of the Patents Act and the Patent Rules.

Once your application has been accepted for filing, you'll be given a number and filing date. Eighteen months after filing your application, the patent office will make your application documents open to the public.

Your application won't be automatically examined; you have to formally request an examination. This request must be made within five years of the filing date. The examination process itself can take two to three years.

If you haven't yet completed your invention and are concerned that others might patent it, filing an application with a description of the invention as far as it has been developed offers you some protection. Competitors will likely refrain from infringing on your invention after your application is published, because you could claim retroactive compensation if you are eventually granted a patent. Also, patents are given to the inventor who first files an application, so you want to file as soon as practicable because a competitor may also be on the same track.

Preparing and following through on a patent application is a complex task. The first thing that must be done is to search existing patents to see if a similar invention has already been patented. If so, there's no point in continuing. Also, the legal scope of the patent protection must be fixed. It's therefore recommended that you consult a lawyer who is a trained patent agent.

The rights conferred by a Canadian patent don't apply in foreign countries. You must apply separately for new patent rights in each country.

5.4.b   Copyrights

The Canadian Copyright Act recognizes the exclusive right of an author to reproduce every original literary, musical, dramatic, and artistic work he or she creates. This includes books, maps, lyrics, musical scores, paintings, sculptures, films, computer programs, photographs, plays, and television and radio programs. Copyright means the right to copy, and the author or owner is the only person who may copy his or her work (or allow someone else to do so).

The author must be a Canadian citizen, a British subject, or a citizen of a country belonging to the Berne Copyright Convention when the work was produced. The author's rights are recognized as existing once he or she has produced the work. This exclusive right lasts for the life of the author plus 50 years after the author's death.

When you create an original work, you automatically obtain copyright in Canada; you don't have to register a copyright. However, registration can be useful proof of ownership.

If you wish to register a copyright, you must send your application to the Copyright office (at the Canadian Intellectual Property office) on the prescribed form. You must state your name, give the title of the work, and submit a registration fee, which is a one-time expense. The registration process normally takes four weeks, after which you'll receive an official certificate.

5.4.c   Trademarks

The Trademarks Act governs trademark registration in Canada. Trademark registration gives you the exclusive right to distinguish your wares or services through words, symbols, or designs.

Registration, although advisable, isn't compulsory (except in the case of precious metals). However, a registered mark is more easily protected than an unregistered trademark. Registration is proof of ownership.

A trademark lasts for 15 years and is renewable every 15 years afterward. The Trademarks Act outlines the types of symbols that can and cannot be used.

The application may be submitted by you — the owner of the trademark — or your authorized agent. The registration process involves a preliminary search, your application, examination of your application by the trademarks office (at the Canadian Intellectual Property office), publication of the application, time for challenges to your application, and registration (if there's no opposition).

5.4.d   Industrial designs

An industrial design is any original shape, pattern configuration, or ornamentation applied to a finished article. Examples include the shape of a sofa or the ornamentation on the handle of a knife. The article must be made by an industrial process, and may be made by hand, tool, or machine.

If your design is an original work of art, it's automatically protected under the Copyright Act, and you can register it as such. But once you use it as a model or pattern to make 50 or more manufactured articles, it's usually considered an industrial design, which can only be protected under the Industrial Design Act.

An industrial design may be registered in Canada if the design isn't identical or similar to others registered. The design must be registered within one year of "publication," that is, within one year from the time the design has been made public or offered for commercial use. Registration provides you with exclusive right to the design for up to ten years.

To register a design, you must file a drawing and description with the industrial design office (at the Canadian Intellectual Property office), together with the appropriate fees. A search will be made of earlier designs to determine if the design is novel.

5.4.e Integrated circuit topographies

The federal Integrated Circuit Topography Act covers what is known as integrated circuit topographies. Topographies are the original three-dimensional configurations of the electronic circuits used in microchips and semiconductor chips.

Registration gives the legal owner of an electronic circuit exclusive rights over the copying of the topography and the commercial use of the circuit. The creator is usually the legal owner, but if you've designed the circuit as part of an employment contract, your employer may be the legal owner.

Registration complements any patent protection you may have obtained for the circuit itself and lasts for ten years. The application is fairly simple to prepare. Send your application and a $200 filing fee to the Registrar of Integrated Circuit Topographies at the Canadian Intellectual Property office.

5.5 Product standards

Any product you make for sale in Canada has to meet certain standards to ensure that it's safe and to protect the consumer against faulty construction and misleading sales practices. Your product may therefore have to be inspected by one of the following organizations:

(a) *Standards Council of Canada.* There are standards for everything from very simple products to the most complex. The Standards Council of Canada oversees the National Standards System and accredits the organizations that can develop and test product standards.

For example, the Canadian General Standards Board sets standards for products as diverse as hair-dryers and mobile homes. Most electrical goods must conform to its standards. For information, contact:

Canadian General
Standards Board
Ottawa, ON K1A 1G6
Telephone: (819) 956-0894

You can also check the Canadian Standards Association Web site at <www.csa-international.org> to find the testing laboratory nearest you.

The Underwriters Laboratories of Canada sets standards for fire protection equipment, building materials, marine products, and related products. Its Web site is <www.ulc.ca>.

(b) *Health Canada.* The Health Protection Branch of Health Canada is responsible for setting the standards and managing the health risk associated with selling, manufacturing and importing foods, drugs, cosmetics, and medical equipment. Emphasis is placed on the control of plant facilities, ingredients, formulas, and packaging.

For more information, contact:

Health Protection Branch,
Western Region Office
3155 Willingdon Green
Burnaby, BC V5G 4P2
Telephone: (604) 666-3350

5.6 Immigration and citizenship

If you're established in business in a foreign country, but wish to live and establish a business in Canada, you must contact the Canadian immigration representative in your country.

You must apply for permanent resident status while you're still outside Canada. If you satisfy the immigration officer about the feasibility of your business proposal and you meet all other immigration requirements, it's possible you will receive permanent resident status.

Canadian citizenship isn't usually needed for employment in Canada except in certain areas of the civil service and some professions. If you're considering employment that is not just temporary, you must apply for permanent resident status before your arrival in Canada. You can apply for full citizenship after three years' residence in Canada.

Canadian customs regulations allow the duty-free entry of personal property that is owned by people prior to coming to Canada. You may not sell or dispose of these goods within 12 months of your entry without paying duty.

If you plan to bring with you tools or machinery necessary for your business or profession, be sure to make arrangements before you have them shipped. Customs duty and sales tax are applicable to equipment, and you should be aware of the requirements.

Further information on the above may be obtained from the nearest Canadian embassy or consulate. To contact Citizenship and Immigration Canada, write to:

Citizenship and Immigration Canada
Jean Edmonds Tower South, 21st Floor
365 Laurier Avenue West
Ottawa, ON K1A 1L1

In Vancouver, you can call (604) 666-2171; elsewhere in Canada, call toll free 1-888-242-2100.

(See also *Immigrating to Canada*, another title in the Self-Counsel series.)

5.7 Consumer protection

Unfair business practices are strictly regulated by both the federal and provincial governments, and you should be aware of your rights and obligations under the various laws.

In British Columbia, deceptive and unconscionable trade acts and practices between a consumer and supplier are regulated by the Trade Practice Act. High pressure selling can get you into trouble. The Consumer Protection Act also includes general regulations concerning business transactions.

Contact the provincial Consumer Services Division (Ministry of Attorney General) to get as much information as possible about the regulations that govern the way you are supposed to do business. In Greater Vancouver, the number is (604) 660-3570, or 1-888-564-9963 elsewhere in British Columbia. The Consumer Services Division also has regional offices in Victoria, Kelowna, Kamloops, Prince George, and Cranbrook.

The federal Competition Act covers such things as misleading price advertising. For further information, call the Information Centre of the Competition Bureau of Industry Canada at 1-800-348-5358.

7
ALL ABOUT SHARES

A share is a portion of ownership in a company. It represents a proportionate interest in the *net* value of a company (i.e., what would remain if all the company's liabilities to outside creditors were fully paid). The person who owns the share — the shareholder or member — has a number of contractual rights as set out in the articles and memorandum of the company, as well as those rights set out in the Company Act.

1. KINDS OF SHARES

There are two kinds of shares: par value and without par value. Par value simply means someone assigns an arbitrary value for the shares in relation to the worth of the company. It represents an arbitrary sum in exchange for which a share can be issued.

In most cases, you should incorporate with without par value shares. This way, you're not restricted to issuing your shares for a set price, as you would have to do with par value shares.

The price at which you issue without par value shares to yourselves is strictly dependent upon the amount of equity capital you wish to establish. (See chapter 8 for a discussion of why you shouldn't invest a large sum in the equity capital of a corporation.) You may issue the minimum of one share to each subscriber for 1¢ if you wish, and, if there are only two of you, it would mean that your company would start off with 2¢ in its share capital account.

The equation "net worth = value of shares" isn't in any way affected by starting off with par value shares, instead of without par value shares. This equation is always true, and if you wish to invest $1 in a company, it makes no real difference if you buy one par value share for $1 or one hundred without par value shares for 1¢. The value of both types of shares will rise and fall in relation to the net worth of the company.

2. CLASSES OF SHARES

Generally speaking, shares can have innumerable rights and restrictions attached to them. A class of shares is a set of shares that has attached to it rights different from the rights attached to another set of shares.

For example, when you start your business, you, like most people, should incorporate with an issue of "common shares" to all the incorporators, so that all the shareholders of the company have equal rights to vote and receive dividends. Most non-reporting companies in British Columbia incorporate with one class of common shares without par value.

When your company becomes successful, you might, however, wish to create a different class of shares which, when issued to shareholders, would give them the right to receive dividends before holders of any other class of shares, or which have cumulative dividend rights or rights to be redeemed by the company. You might refer to the new class of shares as "preferred" shares to distinguish them from the first group of common shares. Preferred shares typically give their holders a preference on any declared dividends.

Both par value and without par value shares can be issued in different classes. For example, you can have preferred without par value shares and cumulative par value shares.

Remember, however, that it's much easier to add rights and restrictions at a later date rather than attach them now and have to buy them up or strip them later. If, at a later date, you wish to create classes of shares that have different rights attached to them, you should see a lawyer so you can carry out the alterations of your articles correctly and design your capital structure properly to minimize taxes and maximize control.

Most small non-reporting companies have no need for many different classes of shares, so this section probably will not apply to your company in any event. (Large reporting companies usually have many different classes of shares.)

3. ISSUING AND CANCELLING SHARES

The issuing and cancelling of shares is a relatively simple affair because the form of share certificate is already prepared for you (available in the *Incorporation Forms and Disk for BC* kit, available from the publisher of this book).

You should be careful, however, to distinguish between the *initial* issue of shares on incorporation, *subsequent* issues out of the treasury (i.e., from the unissued "pool"), and *transfers* of already-issued shares from one person to another. All three of these dealings involve different operations and are discussed under separate headings below.

The Company Act requires that the company issue a share certificate to the shareholder within one month of issuing shares to that person. (You don't need a separate certificate for each share.) For the average small, non-reporting company, relatively few share certificates will suffice for normal purposes. This is because there are usually only a few shareholders, and each share certificate can represent the total number of shares held by each person.

Share certificates must be manually signed by at least one director or officer. Any other signatures may be printed or mechanically reproduced. Share certificates should be numbered consecutively in the space provided at the top of the certificate. The remaining information needed can be ascertained by closely examining the share certificate in Sample 18.

Whenever possible, share certificates should remain in the minute book, because if they're sent to the individual shareholder, some will inevitably be lost. You'll then be faced with the annoying problem of replacing lost share certificates and proving details of the loss.

To cancel shares, simply write the word "cancelled" across the face of the certificate and staple it shut on top of the tab or stub of the certificate (see Sample 19.)

Finally, you must prepare the appropriate directors' consent resolutions confirming the issuance or cancellation of shares. Actually, there should never be a cancellation unless there is, at the same time, a transfer, so the two would be incorporated into the same resolutions. Examples of consent resolutions showing the initial issue of shares are shown in Sample 17 (see chapter 5).

4. INITIAL ISSUE OR ALLOTMENT OF SHARES

The initial issue of shares can be most simply handled by having all the intended shareholders sign the memorandum and place beside their names the number and kind of shares to be subscribed for (see Sample 6 in chapter 4).

SAMPLE 18
SHARE CERTIFICATE

Company J & J Industries

SHARE CERTIFICATE

Certificate # 1 Class Common No. of Shares 50 Par Value No
Registered Name John Doe
Date entered in
Register of Members June 1 200 -

Cert. #	Class	# of Shares	Par Value	Date Name Entered in Register
1	Common	50	No	June 1, 200 -

This certifies that John Doe
of Anywhere, British Columbia
of Fifty (50) Common Shares,
in the Authorized Capital of

J & J Industries Ltd.

INCORPORATED IN THE PROVINCE OF BRITISH COLUMBIA

is the registered holder

transferable only in the Register of Members, and in accordance with the Articles of the Company, by completion of the Form of Transfer endorsed hereon and surrender of this Certificate.

IN WITNESS WHEREOF the Company has caused this Certificate to be signed by its duly

authorized officer(s) this 29th day of June 200 -

John Doe

President   John Doe

TITLE

TRANSFER OF THESE SHARES IS RESTRICTED

TRANSFER DETAILS

From:
To:
Received (Certificate Number)
this day of 200 -

SAMPLE 19
CANCELLED SHARE CERTIFICATE

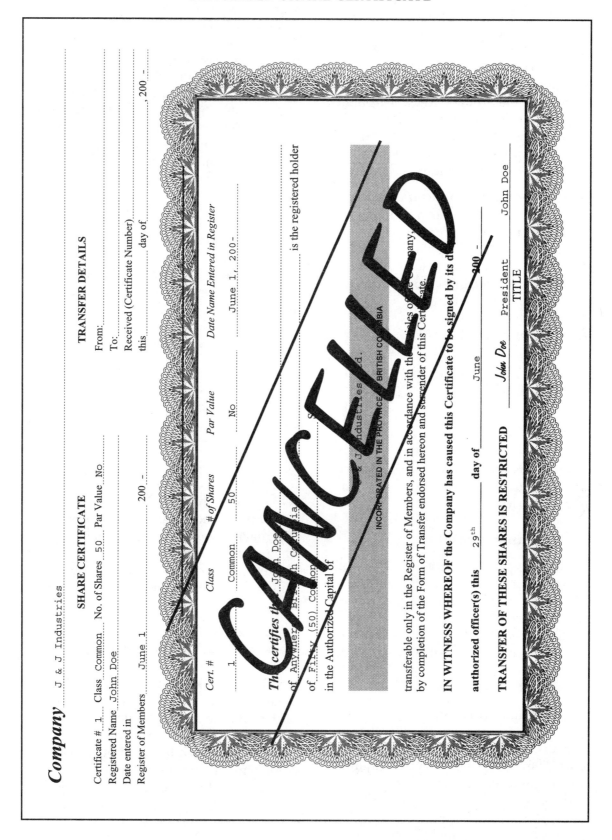

Company J & J Industries

SHARE CERTIFICATE

Certificate # 1 Class Common No. of Shares 50 Par Value No.
Registered Name John Doe
Date entered in
Register of Members June 1 200 -

TRANSFER DETAILS

From:
To:
Received (Certificate Number)
this day of , 200 -

Cert. #	Class	# of Shares	Par Value	Date Name Entered in Register
1	Common	50	No.	June 1, 200 -

This certifies that John Doe
of Anywhere, British Columbia is the registered holder
of Fifty (50) Common shares J & J Industries Ltd.
in the Authorized Capital of INCORPORATED IN THE PROVINCE OF BRITISH COLUMBIA

transferable only in the Register of Members, and in accordance with the Articles of the Company,
by completion of the Form of Transfer endorsed hereon and surrender of this Certificate.

IN WITNESS WHEREOF the Company has caused this Certificate to be signed by its d

authorized officer(s) this 29th day of June 200 -

John Doe John Doe President
TITLE

TRANSFER OF THESE SHARES IS RESTRICTED

CANCELLED

93

The only problem with this method is that the first subscribers are automatically the first directors. If any of your initial shareholders don't wish to be directors, you'll have to file a Notice of Directors with your other incorporation documents. And as all directors have considerable responsibility placed upon them, it would be wise for you to read the section "Duties and Responsibilities of Directors and Officers" in chapter 13, before you subscribe to shares on the memorandum.

In any event, upon incorporation, you still have to prepare a document showing the consent resolutions for electing officers, transferring assets (if applicable), and attending to other miscellaneous transactions, so it only requires an extra clause in this document to document the issuing of the initial shares (see the clause on "Allotment of Shares" in Sample 17).

5. HOW MANY SHARES SHOULD YOU ISSUE?

You can have any number of without par value shares or shares at a par value ranging anywhere from 1¢ to $100 or more per share. However, there are several important points to remember when determining how many shares to issue at the outset.

5.1 Proportion of shares

When issuing shares initially, it's the proportion of shares each shareholder receives that's important, not the number. For example, if you're the only shareholder, you could issue yourself one share at $10 000 each or 10 000 shares at $1 each. Either way, your company ends up with $10 000 and you own 100% of the shares.

If there are two shareholders and they are to own the company equally, the company can issue each shareholder 10 shares or 5 000 shares — the number is unimportant as long as the equal proportion is maintained.

5.2 More shares rather than less

In some cases, it may be more convenient to issue a larger number of shares rather than just a few (i.e., several thousand rather than a few dozen). This way, it will be easier to sell any of these shares to another person, because each share will have a lower value. Similarly, it will be easier for a newcomer to your company to subscribe for shares from the company treasury, since each share will have a lower value than if only a few were issued.

For example, if you and your partner each invest $1 000 in your company, you could issue to each of you 10 shares at $100 each or 10 000 shares at 10¢ each. However, if you chose to issue shares at $100 each, a share purchaser with only $50 couldn't buy any shares.

5.3 Don't issue all shares

There's no need in most simple incorporation situations to immediately issue all the shares. The unissued shares remain in the company treasury and belong to it until it becomes necessary to issue them to new shareholders.

Although you may feel that issuing and selling many shares is a good idea because it will bring money into your corporation and make it worth more, this isn't correct. The number of shares issued doesn't affect the real value of your company. The simplified examples in Samples 20 and 21 illustrate this.

In Sample 20, the company issued 100 shares at $1 each. The company has earned $4 000 to date. Therefore, its total net worth is $100 (original investment) + $4 000 (earnings) for a total of $4 100. However, as $100 of this amount is shareholders' money and it's really a matter of transferring it from one hand to the other, it shouldn't be included in determining the value of the corporation for the shareholders. So, deduct

BALANCE SHEET
(Where 100 shares are issued)

J & J INDUSTRIES LIMITED

Assets		Liabilities	
Cash	$ 100	Note to the bank	$2 000
Inventory	4 000	Shareholder loan	3 000
Building	5 000		
Total assets	$9 100	Total liability	$5 000
		Net worth	
		Capital stock authorized	
		10 000 shares	
		Issued 100 shares at $1 each	100
		John Doe 50 shares	
		Jack Doe 50 shares	
		Retained earnings	4 000
		Total equity	4 100
		Total liability and equity	$9 100

Note: The corporation has earned $4 000 to date. Each share is worth $41 (total net worth divided by 100) but as $100 of this amount is shareholders' money, and it is really a matter of transferring it from one hand to the other, it really should not be included in determining the value of the corporation from the shareholders' point of view. Therefore, if the corporation were liquidated tomorrow, it would be worth $4 000 in net returns to the shareholders.

BALANCE SHEET
(Where 10 000 shares are issued)

J & J INDUSTRIES LIMITED

Assets		Liabilities	
Cash	$10 000	Note to the bank	$2 000
Inventory	4 000	Shareholder loan	3 000
Building	5 000		
Total assets	$19 000	Total liability	$5 000
		Net worth	
		Capital stock authorized	
		10 000 shares	
		Issued 10 000 shares at $1 each	10 000
		John Doe 5 000 shares	
		Jack Doe 5 000 shares	
		Retained earnings	4 000
		Total equity	14 000
		Total liability and equity	$19 000

Note: If the business is wound up, John and Jack Doe's shares are worth $14 000, but $10 000 of this is their own money. Therefore, the net return would again be $4 000.

the original $100 investment from the net worth. If the corporation were liquidated tomorrow, it would actually be worth $4 000 in net returns to the shareholders.

In Sample 21, the company issued 10 000 shares at $1 each. The company has earned $4 000 to date. Therefore, its total net worth is $10 000 (original investment) + $4 000 (earnings) for a total of $14 000. But, again, as described above, we deduct the original investment of $10 000 from the net worth, leaving the same $4 000 in net returns to the shareholders if the company were liquidated tomorrow.

On a net return basis, the company is worth the same whether it issues 100 or 10 000 shares.

Also, retaining some shares in your treasury allows flexibility as your company grows and changes.

Consider the situation where a new shareholder will be joining the corporation. If you'd issued all the shares in the company, you would have to transfer a percentage of each existing shareholder's shares to the new shareholder. In order to do this, you could easily end up with fractional shares.

For example, say John and Jack Doe are the only shareholders in their company and each holds 50 shares. They decide to bring in Helen as an equal shareholder. To do this, both Jack and John have to sell 16 2/3 shares to Helen and each party is left with 33 1/3 shares — an awkward situation.

If, however, there were still unissued shares remaining in the treasury, you could either issue extra shares to the existing shareholders that they could in turn sell to the new shareholder, or simply issue new shares directly to the new shareholder.

So, in the example above, the company could issue 25 more shares each to John and Jack, who could then sell those to Helen, leaving all three shareholders with equal shareholdings of 50 shares each.

Now, John and Jack could choose to sell the new shares to Helen at a higher price, but if they did so, they might trigger capital gains tax. If they chose to sell the shares to Helen for the same price as they paid, the tax department might consider that a taxable benefit to Helen and tax her.

If the shares were issued directly from the treasury to Helen, no tax would be triggered, but, of course, John and Jack would make no actual profit from bringing Helen in, because the money paid by Helen goes into the corporation and not to John or Jack.

Yet another major reason for not issuing all the shares is that even if they were issued at 1¢ each, if 10 000 shares were available, it would cost the shareholders another $100 that has to be put into the company's bank account at the time of incorporation. There's no advantage in financing the company by this method.

6. SUBSEQUENT ISSUE OR ALLOTMENT OF SHARES

6.1 At what price?

Questions often arise over what price the shares should be valued at when a new partner or shareholder is buying into an existing company.

In a reporting company, where the shares are publicly traded, there is no problem establishing the price. In a non-reporting company, it's more difficult.

Broadly speaking, the Company Act allows the directors of a non-reporting company to issue new shares at whatever price they wish. Par value shares may not be issued for less than their par value, however. In the case of shares without par value, the directors may determine their price as authorized by part 3.7 of the articles.

6.2 Tax considerations

Most small businesses would rather not hire some outside business consultant to "value" the shares. And if, as is often the case, the new partner or shareholder is brought in because of the expertise he or she can contribute to the business, that person often doesn't pay full market value for the shares.

However, if the shares are issued at less than market value, you should consider the tax implications for the new partners receiving shares in the company.

The Income Tax Act states that if a new shareholder pays less than fair market value for shares, then the balance is called a taxable benefit and must be included in the new shareholder's income for the year in which the shares are received as a capital gain.

Obviously, there are problems for the tax department questioning this type of valuation in a small, non-reporting company. However, should they audit your company's return and reassess the person involved, it's up to the taxpayer to disprove the tax department's position, which is difficult to do.

There are some legal steps around this problem, such as claiming a reserve against the "gain" or having the new shareholder purchase an "option" at a much lower price instead of the shares themselves. But all these steps require some assistance from a professional and really go beyond the scope of this book. If this situation applies to you, you'll need some expert advice.

Note: An employee may buy new shares at any price without being considered to have received a taxable benefit. The only requirement is that the employee keep the shares in his or her name for two years. When the shares are sold, the difference between the actual purchase price and the sale price is a capital gain. This tax advantage offers employees the opportunity to buy a substantial interest in their company for very little money and receive a valuable employee benefit.

6.3 Pro rata basis

The Company Act gives existing shareholders *pre-emptive rights* on new issues of shares. These pre-emptive rights prevent the possibility of a company issuing new shares to water down the rights of minority shareholders.

To allow shareholders these pre-emptive rights, the directors of a non-reporting company must, before allotting new shares, offer them pro rata to the existing shareholders (see section 41 of the Company Act). On a new issue of shares, the existing shareholders have the right to maintain their *proportionate* positions in relation to the other shareholders.

For example, say J & J Industries Ltd. initially allotted 50 shares to John Doe and 50 shares to Jack Doe. If the directors decided to issue a further 200 shares (the directors being, in this case, the same persons) each shareholder would have the right to take up to a further 100 shares.

The practical effect of all this is that each shareholder can maintain his or her position in relation to the other shareholders.

In many cases, because the shareholders and directors are the same persons, all parties will agree to a new issue of shares.

6.4 Consent by existing shareholders

After receiving a subscription for an allotment of a specific number of shares (see Sample 22), existing shareholders must sign a consent and waiver (see Sample 23) before resolutions in writing can be drawn up to allot new shares (see Sample 24).

SAMPLE 22
SUBSCRIPTION

TO: J & J INDUSTRIES LTD.
AND TO: The Directors thereof

The undersigned subscribe for and agree to take Common shares without par value in the capital of the above-named company set opposite our respective names at the price of $0.50 per share and enclose the sums of $50.00 each payable to the company in full payment of the aggregate price of said shares.

DATED this 12th day of September, 200-.

Name | Number of Shares
John Doe | 100 Common shares without par value
Jack Doe | 100 Common shares without par value

John Doe
_____
JOHN DOE

Jack Doe
_____
JACK DOE

SAMPLE 23
CONSENT AND WAIVER FOR ALLOTMENT OF SHARES

J & J INDUSTRIES LTD.
(the "Company")

CONSENT AND WAIVER

In consideration of $100.00, we the undersigned, being all the holders of all the issued common shares in the authorized capital of the Company, consent to the allotment of the following common shares without par value to the following persons at the price of $0.50 each and do waive any and all rights that we may have pursuant to the Memorandum or the Articles of the Company or the "Company Act," (RSBC 1996 Chapter 62 and amending acts) with respect to such allotment:

Name | Number of Shares
John Doe | 100 Common shares without par value
Jack Doe | 100 Common shares without par value

DATED this 12th day of September, 200-.

John Doe
_____
JOHN DOE

Jack Doe
_____
JACK DOE

J & J INDUSTRIES LTD.
(the "Company")

We, the undersigned, being all the directors of the Company, consent in writing to the following resolutions:

WHEREAS subscriptions have been received from the persons listed below for the allotment to them of the number of shares of the class and at the price set opposite their names:

Name	No. and Class of Shares	Price per Share
John Doe	100 Common shares	$0.50
Jack Doe	100 Common shares	$0.50

RESOLVED:

(1) that the Company having received full payment do allot, issue, and deliver to the persons listed above, the number of shares and at the price per share as set opposite their respective names and such shares be declared to be fully paid and non-assessable:

(2) that the following share certificates be issued:

Share certificate #	Name	No. and Class of Shares
3	John Doe	100 Common shares
4	Jack Doe	100 Common shares

and that any director or officer of the Company execute the said share certificates and deliver them to the persons entitled thereto.

DATED this 14th day of September, 200-.

John Doe
JOHN DOE

Jack Doe
JACK DOE

If you plan to issue more shares and if the present shareholders won't sign waivers, you must comply with the procedures detailed in section 41 of the Company Act.

Section 41(3) directs that an offer must be made in writing to each shareholder specifying the number of shares and time for acceptance. The time for acceptance must not be less than seven days but may be longer at the discretion of the directors.

Section 41(4) allows the directors to sell the shares to whoever they wish if the time lapses with no notice of acceptance or they receive a notice declining the offer from one or more shareholders. However, the directors cannot sell to other people on terms that are more favourable than those offered originally to the existing shareholders.

Directors may not issue fractional shares, or shares that haven't been fully paid for in cash or past services. A promissory note isn't sufficient.

7. TRANSFER OF SHARES

This refers to the simple transfer of issued shares from one shareholder to one or more other shareholders.

Transfers are regulated by the company's articles; our model set deals with transfers in detail in part 24. Basically, as in a new issue of shares, part 24 states that the remaining shareholders have the right of first refusal to buy the seller's shares and that they have the right to buy them on a pro rata basis. If the remaining shareholders decline to buy the offered shares, they should sign a consent and waiver as shown in Sample 25.

At this point, the seller may do one of the following:

(a) Decline to sell the shares not accepted

(b) Offer the remaining shares (if any) to the shareholders who accepted the first offer, again on a pro rata basis

SAMPLE 25
CONSENT AND WAIVER FOR TRANSFER OF SHARES

TO: J & J INDUSTRIES LTD.
AND TO: The directors thereof

The undersigned, being all the registered holders of shares in the capital of the company, irrevocably waive any and all right to be offered any of the shares which the directors propose to transfer as follows:

Transferor	Transferee	Number and class of share
John Doe	Jean Doe	50 Common shares
Jack Doe	Jean Doe	50 Common shares

Dated the 3rd day of August, 200-.

John Doe
JOHN DOE

Jack Doe
JACK DOE

(c) Sell the remaining shares (if any) to third parties (persons other than the remaining shareholders), but he or she cannot sell them on more favourable terms than contained in the original offer to the other shareholders

Part 24 outlines the procedure in further detail. The shareholder who is selling shares completes the transfer form on the back of the share certificate (see Sample 26). A directors' resolution transferring the shares is then prepared (see Sample 27), along with the new share certificate. **Note:** Check the new share certificates to make sure the number of shares they represent equal the number of shares represented by the cancelled share certificates.

For example, say John Doe owns 150 common shares of J & J Industries Ltd., represented by share certificate number 1 for 50 common shares and share certificate number 3 for 100 common shares. Jack Doe owns 150 common shares of J & J Industries Ltd., represented by share certificate number 2 for 50 common shares and share certificate number 4 for 100 common shares. John Doe transfers the 50 shares represented by share certificate number 3 to Jean Doe, and Jack Doe transfers the 50 shares represented by his share certificate number 4 to Jean Doe.

If the new shareholder is also going to be appointed a director, a consent to act as a director (see Sample 28) and a members' consent resolution (see Sample 29) are also prepared, and a Notice of Directors is sent to the Registrar of Companies (see chapter 13).

In many cases, an issue and transfer of shares will take place at the same time, especially when a new "partner" shareholder is being brought into the company and the existing shareholders wish to realize a capital gain on the sale of part of their business. In this case, the procedures regarding consents and notices have to be complied with, but the resolutions of directors that confirm the issue and transfer can be combined into one.

Finally, the above discussion on tax considerations regarding the subsequent issue or allotment of shares also applies to transfers. If in doubt about tax ramifications, always consult a tax expert.

8. REDEMPTION OF SHARES

Your company is empowered to redeem or buy back shares that have a right of redemption attached to them. But it must purchase its own shares in accordance with the provisions of sections 236 and 237.

Section 236 provides that the company must not repurchase or redeem shares when the company is insolvent or if such action would cause the company to become insolvent. Section 237 states that a non-reporting company must offer to purchase its shares from shareholders on a pro rata basis the same way it must issue shares on a pro rata basis.

If your company is considering the purchase of some of its shares to reduce its capital base, professional advice should be sought because of the tax ramifications of such a purchase.

101

SAMPLE 26
SHARE TRANSFER FORM
(On back of share certificate)

CERTIFICATE

FOR

One hundred (100) Common   SHARES

REGISTERED IN THE NAME OF

John Doe

CAPITAL

J & J Industries Ltd.

I, John Doe

of   111A Street, Vancouver, BC

in consideration of the sum of $1.00

Dollars paid to me by   Jean Doe

of   333C Street, Vancouver, BC

(hereinafter called the "Transferee"), do hereby transfer to the Transferee

fifty(50)Common   Shares in the undertaking called

J & J Industries Ltd.

to hold unto the Transferee, Jean Doe, and her executors, administrators, and assigns, subject to the several conditions on which I held the same at the time of the execution hereof, and the Transferee in taking delivery hereof takes the said shares subject to the conditions aforesaid.

As Witness my hand the 3rd day of August AD, 200 –

TRANSFEROR *John Doe*

WITNESS *Walter Witness*

J & J INDUSTRIES LTD.

The undersigned, being all the directors of the company, consent to and adopt in writing the following resolutions:

TRANSFER OF SHARES

RESOLVED that a proper instrument of transfer having been received, the following transfer of shares be approved:

Transferor	Transferee	Number and class of share
John Doe	Jean Doe	50 Common shares without par value
Jack Doe	Jean Doe	50 Common shares without par value

CANCELLATION OF SHARE CERTIFICATES

RESOLVED that pursuant to the foregoing transfer of shares, the following share certificates be cancelled:

Share certificate #	Name	Number and class of shares
3	John Doe	100 Common shares without par value
4	Jack Doe	100 Common shares without par value

ISSUE OF NEW SHARE CERTIFICATES

RESOLVED that pursuant to the foregoing transfer of shares, the following share certificates be issued:

Share certificate #	Name	Number and class of shares
5	John Doe	50 Common shares without par value
6	Jack Doe	50 Common shares without par value
7	Jean Doe	100 Common shares without par value

RESOLVED that a director of the company is authorized to execute and deliver the above share certificates.

RESOLVED that the appropriate entries be made in the company's Register of Members and Register of Transfers.

DATED the 3rd day of August, 200-.

John Doe

JOHN DOE

Jack Doe

JACK DOE

CONSENT TO ACT AS DIRECTOR

I, John Doe, of 111 A Street, Anywhere, BC; consent to act as director of J & J INDUSTRIES LTD. This consent is effective until revoked.

John Doe
_____
JOHN DOE

DATED as of the 1st day of June, 200-.

CONSENT RESOLUTIONS OF MEMBERS APPOINTING A NEW DIRECTOR

J & J INDUSTRIES LTD.
(the "Company")

We, the undersigned, being all the members of the Company, consent in writing to the following resolutions:

1.   RESOLVED that the number of directors of the Company be changed from two (2) to three (3).

2.   RESOLVED that Jean Doe be appointed as a director of the Company effective the 15th day of June, 200-, such person having consented in writing to act as a director of the Company.

DATED as of the 3rd day of June, 200-

John Doe
_____
JOHN DOE

Jack Doe
_____
JACK DOE

8
FINANCING YOUR COMPANY

After a new corporation is organized, it may require financing to begin operations. There are three common methods of financing a company:

- By shareholder loan

- By share purchase

- By borrowing capital from a bank or other non-shareholder source

1.   SHAREHOLDER LOAN

The easiest way to raise money for your company is by shareholder loan.

Capital loaned to the company can be recovered at any time, tax free. A loan to the company repaid to a shareholder isn't taxable income to the shareholder. However, the interest earned on the loan is taxable.

Another advantage to a shareholder loan is that the loan ranks equally with other creditors when dividing up the remainder of the assets on the dissolution or bankruptcy of the company. You're more likely to recover your money if you've loaned money to the company as opposed to using it to buy shares.

If you or another shareholder want to loan money to your company, simply write the company a cheque, and make a note on the cheque and bank deposit slip that it is a shareholder loan. The cheque stub will then show the information for your accountant or bookkeeper to make the proper entries in your ledgers.

It's always a good idea to draw up a promissory note or demand note recording the amount of the loan and the interest, if any, payable on it. Your promissory note should state whether the amount of money is to be payable whenever the lender calls for it (a "demand note") or is to be paid off over a period of time in installments.

An example of a demand note is shown in Sample 30. They're quite simple to draw up on your own, or you can purchase the preprinted *Promissory Note* form-and-disk kit available from the publisher. But be sure to read them over carefully before using them. Be certain that a fixed sum is payable on a certain date or at a certain time. The making of the promissory note by the corporation should be approved in either a directors' resolution or in the minutes of a directors' meeting. The note and the approving resolution or minutes would then be filed in the company's minute book.

2.   SHARE PURCHASE

A second method of raising money for the company is by issuing and selling shares to yourself or someone else.

If you're going to be the investor, however, there are definite disadvantages to capitalizing a business through the purchase of shares, especially with a high-risk business being operated by a newly incorporated company.

Money invested in shares cannot be easily recovered while the company is operating. Any recovery must be achieved through wages or dividends, which are taxable in the recipient's hands. Another disadvantage is that if the company collapses, repayment to the shareholders for money invested in shares ranks behind any kind of

---

$2 000   September 30, 200-

ON DEMAND after the above date the company promises to pay to the order of JOHN DOE at Vancouver, British Columbia, TWO THOUSAND DOLLARS ($2 000) with interest at the rate of fifteen percent (15%) per annum, as well after as before maturity, FOR VALUE RECEIVED.

J & J INDUSTRIES LIMITED

Per: "JOHN DOE"
President

"JACK DOE"
Secretary

---

loan, including a shareholder loan. Common shareholders rarely see any proceeds when a company goes bankrupt.

On the positive side, if you need to borrow money to buy the shares, the interest on money borrowed will generally be tax deductible as being "for the purpose of earning income from property."

Also, if the investors will be other businesspeople — not you — it might be more advantageous for your company to sell them shares rather than borrow money from them (see the third option discussed in section **3.** below). By selling them shares —

(a)   the company has no corporate obligation to repay the money unless and until the company is dissolved, and

(b)   the company's balance sheet will appear stronger with more money in the equity column and less in the debt column.

3.   BORROWING CAPITAL

The third option for financing your company is to find a bank or other lender who will loan money to the company. However, lenders are reluctant to loan money directly to small or newly incorporated businesses without taking personal guarantees from the shareholders. This in effect cancels the main benefit to incorporating, which is limited liability. If you choose to have the company take out a loan, only the company is able to take the interest deduction, but the company benefits only if it makes a profit.

9
TRANSFERRING ASSETS TO YOUR COMPANY

1. TAX WRITE-OFFS

Should you transfer assets to your new company to obtain tax write-offs? Many people who incorporate believe that from the point of view of depreciation and expenses, it's better for a company to own assets than an individual. This really isn't true.

Take, for example, the company car. If the company owns the car and you use it for business purposes, the company can deduct operating and depreciation expenses as a valid business expense.

Now if you also use the company car for pleasure, this value is calculated and added to your taxable income as a benefit received (i.e., it's not a free benefit to you). The Income Tax Act currently states that if you use a company car for pleasure, you must include in your personal income an amount equal to 2% per month of the purchase price of the vehicle, or two-thirds of the lease cost if it's leased by your company. If, however, your personal use of the vehicle is less than 1 000 kilometres per month, the standby charge is reduced.

The theory is that you're entitled to use a company vehicle on company business, and the company is entitled to deduct expenses while the vehicle is used in this manner. Your use of the car for other than company business is a taxable benefit to you, and the company may not deduct expenses while the vehicle is used for the pleasure of one of its employees.

On the other hand, if you own the vehicle and use it in the course of employment with a company, you could deduct the employment portion of operating expenses and depreciation from your personal income.

The important thing to remember is that both the company and the individual are entitled to deduct legitimate expenses incurred in the use of such assets, and where you have a small, non-reporting company — really an "incorporated partnership" — in which employees and shareholders are the same persons, it makes little difference whether the company or the individual receives the benefit of these write-offs.

There may be a slight difference, depending on the individual situation, because of the variance in individual and corporate tax rates. However, this usually isn't significant enough to justify a wholesale transfer of assets into the company.

2. BENEFITS

There are, however, benefits to be gained from transferring assets into the company at the time of incorporation.

First, the transfer psychologically "locks" the partners into the company — each makes a commitment to the new venture by "selling" an equal amount of assets to the company.

Second, it makes the accounting easier. It's simplest for the company to own the asset and deduct depreciation and operating expenses. If an employee owns the asset and rents it to the company, both the employee and the company will have to keep records of expenses.

3. AVOIDING PROVINCIAL SALES TAX

Normally, if a company buys an asset, it must pay provincial sales tax. However, you may transfer assets into a newly incorporated corporation without having to pay provincial sales tax if certain criteria are met:

(a) First, you must "wholly own and control" the new company at the time and continue to own it for at least eight months after the transfer. "Wholly own and control" means you own at least 95% of the outstanding shares of each class of the company's share capital (or, if you just have one class of shares, for example, common shares, then 95% of the common shares).

(b) Second, the business assets being transferred must be "tax paid" assets, that is, you've already paid provincial sales tax on the asset when you originally bought it.

(c) Third, you must transfer the assets to the new company before it starts to do business.

4. OTHER FEDERAL TAX ISSUES

4.1 Non-arm's length transfers

If you want to roll over an existing business into a company, or are incorporating your sole proprietorship and selling assets to the new company, you have to be careful to avoid certain federal tax complications. This is because, under the law, you and the company that you control are not dealing at "arm's length." In other words, you're not strangers to each other, and the potential for setting up artificial transactions is something the tax department watches out for.

So, when a sale is made in a non-arm's length transaction, the Income Tax Act requires the selling price to be at fair market value.

In situations where you've been depreciating assets for tax purposes, this can lead to your being personally liable for tax through the recapture of capital cost allowance.

For example, say you've been operating a proprietorship that owns a delivery van valued on the books at $2 000. Perhaps in reality, this van is worth $3 000. You must value the van at that price when you sell it to your company. This would create a recapture situation of $1 000, which would have to be included in your income in the year that the transfer was made and on which you would have to pay taxes.

4.2 Deferring tax

To avoid the situation mentioned above, there is a special section of the Income Tax Act (section 85) which provides for a "rollover" election. Section 85 of the Income Tax Act says you can choose a tax-free rollover of property.

This allows you to defer tax on the recapture and capital gains by electing to transfer the property to your company at its cost or undepreciated capital cost balance. The tax is deferred until the company sells the property to some other person or organization.

So, in the example above, you'd elect to transfer the delivery van to your company at a value of $2 000 instead of the fair market value of $3 000. Later, the company would pay the tax that's been deferred when it sells the van to someone else.

4.3 Real estate

There's a similar provision for the sale of real estate. The forms involved are easy to follow, but the decisions regarding the value of the assets you are transferring to the company are sometimes complicated. So, if you're in the situation where you are selling real estate that you previously

108

owned (or assets that have been depreciated for tax purposes), you should consult your accountant first.

5. DOCUMENTING THE TRANSFER

In any transfer of an asset, keep in mind that you must have adequate proof of the transfer for the federal (income) and provincial (social services) tax departments.

The whole transaction can be reviewed by the income tax department, and transfers of assets at inflated values are usually caught sooner or later. Sometimes the tax people may want an independent appraisal, and if you're able to produce proof of the appraised value, it will greatly strengthen your case.

As far as any car, truck, or other self-propelled industrial equipment that falls under the Motor Vehicles Act is concerned, you'll require documentation in the consent resolutions, plus the usual motor vehicle transfer forms.

To obtain the tax exemption for motor vehicles, you must visit your local Consumer Taxation Branch of the British Columbia Government, and take along your consent resolutions evidencing the transfer. They will issue you an exemption form and you may then go to the Motor Vehicle Branch and complete the transfer forms.

Other assets may be transferred by simply recording the fact in the resolutions of a meeting of directors. If there are a great many items and/or a large amount of money involved, you should draw up a Bill of Sale and file a copy in the company minute book. You can purchase a pre-printed *Bill of Sale* forms-and-disk package from the publisher.

6. FINANCING THE TRANSACTIONS

When you sell your asset to your company, the company must give something back in return as a payment for the debt, called "consideration." The consideration must be equal to the fair market value of the property transferred.

As part of the consideration, you must receive at least one share of the company. You could receive $1 000 worth of shares if you transferred an asset worth $1 000 to the company. Or you could get a $1 share and a promise by the company to pay you back $999 as evidenced by a demand note (see below).

In many cases, it's better to receive a debt obligation (the second alternative above), rather than shares in exchange for your asset. This way, when the company pays off its debts, you can receive the money tax free as the repayment of your loan. But if you receive shares, your assets are forever tied up in the company and you'll receive no direct benefits, unless the company is wound up and the assets are sold at a profit, which is highly unlikely.

The most common form of payment is the demand note, as shown in Sample 30 (see chapter 8). A note like this should be prepared on behalf of the company in favour of each person transferring assets into the company. As you can see from Sample 30, John Doe is entitled to "demand" payment at any time.

But what's to stop Mr. Doe from demanding payment immediately? First, he's not likely to demand payment unless he knows there are sufficient funds in the company's bank account to pay him. Second, if he had to sue, it would be tantamount to suing himself since he is the part owner of the company.

So, a demand note payable to a shareholder or director of an incorporated partnership is a relatively safe proposition. Usually an informal agreement between the working shareholders (i.e., "incorporated partners") about where and when the notes should be presented for payment is quite sufficient.

If the company pays interest on the note to Mr. Doe, he has to pay tax on it. Interest payments made to the holder of the note are taxable in the noteholder's hands. The principal amount isn't taxable, however, as it's analogous to the repayment of a loan made to the company.

7.   RISKS

There is one major taxable risk in transferring assets to a company. If the company goes bankrupt or has judgements registered against it, the assets may be subject to seizure by the trustee in bankruptcy or the judgement creditor. If this happens, the debt owed to you by the company would be relegated to general creditor status, and you'd have to share in the proceeds of the resale of the assets along with the other creditors.

This happens infrequently, though, because you can usually foresee these events, in which case you may make demand on your note and seize the asset(s) in the event of the company's non-payment. In doing this, you should be aware of a little-known law called the Fraudulent Preferences Act. It says that no one may transfer or convey property with the intention of defeating creditors. There's a three-month time limit from the date of the transfer within which the creditor must apply to upset the transfer of the property from your company to you.

If you intend to transfer many valuable assets, it would be wise to transfer the goods by way of a chattel mortgage or conditional sales agreement. You are then elevated to the level of secured creditor if there are other claims made on the assets. The mortgage or conditional sales agreement must be registered in the Companies office, the particulars of the mortgage inserted in your register of debentures, and a copy of the mortgage filed in your minute book. A lawyer will draw up either agreement for you.

10
BUY-SELL AGREEMENTS

A buy-sell agreement is simply an agreement among the shareholders of a company that, on the happening of a certain event (usually the death or resignation of one of the partner shareholders), one or more of the remaining shareholders will buy the shares of the deceased or departing person. The purpose of the agreement is to enable the existing shareholders to retain control of the company.

The form of buy-sell agreement shown in Sample 31 is a very simple one and is provided only as a sample of what might be included in one. If you wish to enter into a buy-sell agreement, you should obtain legal advice. Still, this chapter will alert you to the issues involved in buy-sell agreements. You may also wish to make use of the *Buy-Sell Agreement* forms-and-disk kit available from the publisher.

1. WHY YOU NEED AN AGREEMENT

The death of a shareholder in a closely-held, non-reporting company creates a serious situation for both the estate of the deceased shareholder and the surviving shareholders of the company.

From the point of view of the estate of the deceased shareholder, the shares of the company held by the deceased shareholder may have no market, as outsiders will seldom buy such shares, unless the business is an established one and they are able to buy the majority interest in the company. The only persons who may be interested in buying the shares may be the surviving shareholders. But, if the deceased had a minority interest in the company, the surviving shareholders would retain control anyway. Thus they would have no real interest in buying the shares and, therefore, have the power to force the estate to sell the shares at bargain prices.

From the point of view of the company, it may be very important to prevent the sale of the shares by the estate to a stranger or to someone with whom the remaining shareholders don't get along, or to prevent the shares from being held by the beneficiaries of the deceased shareholder.

The death of a shareholder in a close corporation with no prior agreement on the disposition of the shares may also adversely affect the credit position of the company, because of the uncertainty as to the future of the business.

The only effective solution to these problems is for all the shareholders of the company to enter into a buy-sell agreement. Under this type of agreement, the estate of a deceased shareholder is obligated to sell, and the surviving shareholders are obligated to purchase, all the shares of the deceased at a specified price or at a price to be determined under the agreement.

Buy-sell agreements have the advantage of relative simplicity, except where there are more than two or three parties, when this type of agreement can become very complicated.

However, buy-sell agreements raise two major issues:

    (a)   The funding of the purchase of the shares

Buy-Sell Agreement

BUY-SELL AGREEMENT made the_____ day of_____, 20_____,

between_____
(name)

of the city of_____ in the province of_____

(herein called_____),

and_____
(name)

of the city of_____ in the province of_____

(herein called_____).

WHEREAS:

(1)   The parties own or control all the issued and outstanding shares in_____
_____ Corporation Limited (herein called "the Corporation") as
follows:*(set out shareholdings)*

(2)   The parties desire to provide for their mutual protection if either dies or wishes to
withdraw from the Corporation.

THIS AGREEMENT WITNESSES that the parties covenant and agree as follows:

1.   The parties shall not transfer, encumber, or in any way deal with any of their shares
in the Corporation except as provided for in this agreement.

During the lifetime of the parties

2.   If either_____ or_____
wishes to dispose of his/her shares in the Corporation, he/she (herein called the "Offeror") shall
first offer in writing to sell all his/her shares to the other party (herein called the "Offeree") on
the following terms and conditions.

3.   The offer shall contain:

(a)   an offer to sell all the shares of the Corporation owned or controlled by the Offeror (herein called "all his/her shares" or "the shares") at the arbitrary price stipulated in the offer;

(b)   an offer to purchase all the shares of the Corporation owned or controlled by the Offeree (herein called "all his/her shares" or "the shares") at the same price;

(c)   an undertaking to close the purchase or sale on a date fixed not less than _[eighty (80)]_ days and not more than _[one hundred (100)]_ days from the service of the offer on the Offeree at the time and place fixed in the offer.

4.   If the Offeree accepts the offer to sell under paragraph 3, the Offeror (herein called "the Vendor") shall sell and transfer all his/her shares to the Offeree (herein called "the Purchaser") who shall purchase and pay for them on the date and at the place stated in the offer for the arbitrary price stipulated in the offer.

5.   If the Offeree accepts the offer to purchase under paragraph 3(b), the Offeree (herein called "the Vendor") shall sell all his/her shares to the Offeror (herein called "the Purchaser") who shall purchase and pay for them on the date and at the place stated in the offer for the arbitrary price stipulated in the offer.

6.   If the Offeree does not accept either of the alternative offers in accordance with the provisions, he/she shall be deemed to have accepted the Offeror's offer to sell all his/her shares to the Offeree and the Offeree (herein called "the Purchaser") shall purchase and pay for them on the date and at the place stated in the offer for the arbitrary price stipulated in the offer.

7.   At the time set for closing, the Vendor shall deliver to the Purchaser in exchange for the items set out in paragraph 8:

(a)   certificates for all his/her shares duly endorsed in blank for transfer;

(b)   his/her resignation from the board and that of his/her spouse and nominees, if applicable;

(c)   his/her resignation as an employee and that of his/her spouse and members of his/her family who may be in the employ of the Corporation;

(d)   an assignment to the Purchaser of all debts, if any, owing by the Corporation to the Vendor;

(e)   a release of all claims the Vendor has or may have against the Corporation and the Purchaser;

(f)   assignment of all insurance policies on the life of the Purchaser as set out in Appendix A;

(g)   a certified cheque payable to the Purchaser for an amount equal to the aggregate of the cash surrender value of all policies on the life of the Vendor as set out in Appendix A;

(h)   all other documents necessary or desirable in order to carry out the true intent of this agreement.

8.   At the time set for closing, the Purchaser shall deliver to the Vendor in exchange for the items set out in paragraph 7 above:

(a)   a certified cheque payable to the Vendor for the full amount of the arbitrary purchase price of the shares;

(b)   a certified cheque payable to the Vendor for the full amount of any indebtedness owing by the Corporation to the Vendor as recorded on the books of the Corporation and verified by the Corporation's accountant;

(c)   a certified cheque payable to the Vendor for an amount equal to the aggregate of the cash surrender value of all policies on the life of the Purchaser as set out in Appendix A;

(d)   a release by the Corporation of all debts, if any, owing by the Vendor to the Corporation;

(e)   a release of all claims the Corporation and the Purchaser have or may have against the Vendor;

(f)   a release of all guarantees given by the Vendor on behalf of the Corporation;

(g)   all securities, free and clear of all claims, which belong to the Vendor and are lodged with any person (including the Corporation's banks) to secure an indebtedness or credit of the Corporation;

(h)   assignments of all insurance policies on the life of the Vendor as set out in Appendix A;

(i)   all other documents necessary or desirable in order to carry out the true intent of this agreement.

9.   If on the closing date the Vendor neglects or refuses to complete the transaction or does not comply with the procedures herein set out, the Purchaser has the right upon such default (without prejudice to any other rights that he/she may have), upon payment by him/her of the purchase price (plus or minus any adjustments herein provided) to the credit of the Vendor in any chartered bank in the city of_____ (or to the solicitor for the Corporation in trust for, on behalf of, and in the name of the Vendor), to complete the transaction as above. The Vendor hereby irrevocably constitutes the Purchaser his/her true and lawful attorney to complete the said transaction and execute on behalf of the Vendor every document necessary or desirable in that behalf. [If there is more than one vendor, this power of attorney shall apply to both vendors.]

10.   If on the closing date the Purchaser neglects or refuses to complete the transaction, or does not comply with the procedures herein set out, the Vendor has the right upon such default (without prejudice to any other rights that he/she may have) to give to the Purchaser, within ten (10) days after such default, notice that on the twenty-first day after the original closing date, he/she (herein called "the New Purchaser") will purchase from the Purchaser (herein called "the New Vendor") all the shares of the Corporation owned or controlled by the New Vendor, for an amount equal to seventy-five percent (75%) of the purchase price set out in paragraph 8(a) and at the same time fix a new date within thirty (30) days and a time and place for closing; whereupon, on the new date for closing, the New Vendor shall sell all his/her shares to the New Purchaser who shall purchase the same for the new purchase price, and it is expressly agreed that all the terms of this agreement applicable to the closing of the sale and purchase of shares and to the adjustment of purchase price, if any, shall be applicable to the said closing. The New Vendor hereby constitutes the New Purchaser his/her true and lawful attorney to complete the said transaction and execute on behalf of the New Vendor every document necessary or desirable in that behalf. [If there is more than one vendor, this power of attorney shall apply to both vendors.]

11.   No offer hereunder shall be given while another offer is outstanding or a sale pending or until_____ days after any sale is aborted.

After the death of a party

12.   Within_[one hundred (100)]_ days of the death of either_____ or _____ (provided the survivor is alive on the thirtieth day after the death of the first deceased) the survivor (Purchaser) shall purchase and the estate of the deceased (Vendor) shall sell to the survivor all his/her shares owned or controlled by the deceased at the time of his/her death for the most recent price stipulated in the offer.

13. The legal representatives of the deceased shall fix, in writing, a date not more than __[one hundred (100)]__ days from the date of death, a time and a place for the closing of the sale of its shares.

14. At the time set for closing, the Purchaser shall deliver to the Vendor/Estate in exchange for the items set out in paragraph 15:

(a) a certified cheque payable to the Vendor/Estate for the full amount of the purchase price as set out in the offer;

(b) a certified cheque payable to the Vendor/Estate for the full amount of any indebtedness owing by the Corporation to the deceased;

(c) a certified cheque payable to the Vendor/Estate for the amount of the cash surrender value on all insurance policies on the life of the Purchaser listed in Appendix A;

(d) a certified cheque payable to the Vendor/Estate for the amount, if any, by which the aggregate net proceeds received by the Purchaser from the insurers in Appendix A exceeds the aggregate of (a),(b), and (c) above;

(e) a release by the Corporation and the Purchaser of all debts and other claims that they have or may have against the Vendor/Estate;

(f) a release of all guarantees given by the deceased Vendor on behalf of the Corporation;

(g) all securities, free and clear of all claims, belonging to the deceased Vendor which are lodged with any person (including the Corporation's banks) to secure any indebtedness or credit of the Corporation;

(h) all other documents necessary or desirable in order to carry out the true intent of this agreement.

15. At the time set for closing, the Vendor/Estate shall deliver to the Purchaser in exchange for the items set out in paragraph 14:

(a) certificates for all the Vendor's shares duly endorsed for transfer in blank with signature guaranteed by a bank or trust company;

(b) evidence of authority of executors to sign;

(c) succession duty release for the shares if applicable;

(d) resignations from the board and employment of all members of the deceased's family and nominees;

(e) an assignment to the Purchaser of all debts, if any, owing by the Corporation to the Vendor;

(f) a release of all claims the deceased Vendor or his/her Estate has or may have against the Corporation or the Purchaser;

(g) an assignment to the Purchaser of all insurance policies on the life of the Purchaser listed in Appendix A;

(h) all other documents necessary or desirable in order to carry out the true intent of this agreement.

Insurance

16. In order to ensure that all or a substantial part of the purchase price for the shares of the deceased party will be available immediately in cash upon his/her death, each of the parties hereto has procured insurance on the other's life as set out in Appendix A. Additional policies may be taken out for the purposes of this agreement and they shall be added to Appendix A.

17. Each of the parties hereto agrees, throughout the term of this agreement, to maintain and pay the premiums as they fall due on the life insurance policies listed in Appendix A owned by him/her.

18. The insurers set out in Appendix A are hereby authorized and directed to give any party hereto, upon written request, all information concerning the status of the said policies.

19. If any premium on any insurance policy is not paid within __[twenty (20)]__ days after its due date, the party insured shall have the right to pay such premium and be reimbursed by the owner together with interest at the rate of __[two]__ percent per month on the amount so paid in respect of such premium from the overdue payment until the date of reimbursement.

20. Immediately upon the death of one of the parties hereto, the survivor shall proceed as expeditiously as possible to collect the proceeds of the policies on the deceased party, and the legal representatives of the Estate of the deceased party shall apply and expedite the application for letters of administration or letters probate, as may be required.

21. The parties shall not assign, encumber, borrow upon, or otherwise deal with any of the insurance policies set out in Appendix A.

SAMPLE 31 — Continued

General

22. The parties shall not throughout the term of this agreement and until a valid sale of the shares is completed under this agreement do or cause or permit to be done anything out of the normal course of business of the Corporation.

23. Time shall be of the essence of this agreement and everything that relates thereto.

24. The parties agree to execute and deliver any documents necessary or desirable to carry out the true purpose and intent of this agreement.

25. This agreement shall be binding upon and enure to the benefit of the parties hereto and their respective heirs, executors, administrators, and assigns.

IN WITNESS WHEREOF we have set our hands and our seals this_____ day of _____, 20_____.

SIGNED, SEALED, AND DELIVERED   )
in the presence of   )
)
)
_____   )   _____
(Witness signature)   )   *(Signature)*
)
_____   )   _____
(Witness signature)   )   *(Signature)*

Appendix A
_____ **Corporation Limited**
Buy-Sell Agreement

Life insurance policies on the life of_____

owned by_____.

| *Insurer* | *Number* | *Amount* |

Life insurance policies on the life of_____

owned by_____.

| *Insurer* | *Number* | *Amount* |

ALTERNATE VALUATION CLAUSES

Valuation by auditor — Book value at fixed date

The survivor and the executors or administrators of the deceased shall cause a valuation of all other shares of common and preferred stock of the Corporation to be made by the auditors of the Corporation based on the book value of the Corporation on the first day of the month immediately preceding the deceased's death. If within thirty (30) days the survivor and the executors or administrators of the deceased have not signified their approval of the valuation of the shares of the Corporation as determined by the auditors, the value of such shares shall be fixed by a board of three (3) arbitrators selected as follows: the survivor shall select one arbitrator, the executors or administrators of the deceased shall select one arbitrator, and the two so selected shall select the third arbitrator and the decision of a majority of the said arbitrators as to such valuation shall be final.

Book value — Capitalization of fixed assets

To the book value of the shares of the Corporation shall be added an amount equal to [six]   times the difference between the average net profit of the Corporation, after payment of all taxes and dividends for [three]   complete fiscal years of the Corporation immediately preceding the deceased's death, and [ten] percent of the adjusted net asset value of the Corporation as above determined at the date of the deceased's death.

(b)   The valuation of the deceased or departed person's shares

2.   FUNDING THE PURCHASE OF THE SHARES

Usually, the purchase of the shares is funded by business life insurance policies, under which each shareholder insures the lives of his or her fellow shareholders, naming himself or herself as beneficiary of each policy.

The idea is that the surviving shareholders will use the insurance proceeds to buy the shares of the deceased shareholder from the estate of the deceased shareholder.

There are, of course, different types of life insurance and the decision as to which type should be obtained by the parties, the amount of insurance, and other related matters should be made only after consultation with an experienced life insurance underwriter.

3.   VALUING THE DEPARTED PERSON'S SHARES

Valuing the departed person's shares may be dealt with in a number of ways, as no single method of valuation is appropriate to all types of business operations or circumstances. There are four general methods by which shares can be valued:

(a)   By some form of fixed formula (book value, capitalization of earnings, etc., or a combination of two or more of these methods)

(b)   By some form of appraisal or arbitration

(c)   By a fixed dollar amount by agreement among the parties, with or without a provision for periodic revaluation

(d)   By a combination of two or more of these methods

In an incorporated husband and wife business, where the couple is separating, you can divide the shares according to each person's contribution. Ideally, however, a buy-sell agreement should be drawn up that provides that one person should buy up the other according to a predetermined formula. Determining this formula is often the greatest difficulty in making one of these agreements. You may wish to use a coin toss to decide which party is to buy out the other if there are two people who are equally capable of running the business. The proceeds of a cashed-in life insurance policy may be used to finance the purchase.

Whatever the terms of the agreement, it's a good idea to have this matter settled before a marriage breaks up. Many people have made the unfortunate discovery that it's extremely difficult to make maintenance payments to someone out of earnings derived from a company that is disrupted by disagreements between its directors. Too often, if no agreement is reached, the company is wound up and both parties experience unnecessary economic loss.

By adopting a buy-sell agreement, the parties are bound to resolve this messy situation according to a predetermined formula — one that can be enforced in the courts if need be.

11
ANNUAL GENERAL MEETING AND ANNUAL REPORT

1. ANNUAL GENERAL MEETING

The Company Act requires a company to hold an annual general meeting within 15 months of its incorporation. Afterward, annual general meetings must be held at least once each calendar year and within 13 months of the previous meeting.

Although it's good practice to hold regular annual meetings, this legal requirement amounts to a bothersome formality for many non-reporting companies. It's therefore possible to avoid this requirement by consent resolution.

If all the shareholders entitled to attend and vote at the annual general meeting consent in writing to all the business that would be discussed and transacted at that meeting, you don't have to hold a meeting. The meeting is deemed to have been held on the date the consent resolution is signed. Instead of a meeting, you can have all the shareholders sign the consent resolutions shown in Samples 32 and 33, and enter these in the minute book instead.

At each annual general meeting, a non-reporting company must appoint an auditor, unless all shareholders consent in writing to a resolution waiving the appointment of one. Most non-reporting companies don't need the services of an auditor and generally waive the appointment (see the first option in Sample 32).

However, you may want to consider taking on the extra expense of an audit in the following circumstances:

(a) When you or a co-owner aren't involved in the day-to-day running of the company

(b) When the shareholders aren't the same people as the managers

(c) When there are a large number of shareholders and an audit would reassure everyone of the company's position and protect the officers who are making accounting decisions

(d) When the volume of business transactions is so large that it's hard for one person to keep on top of it all

(e) When considerable borrowing is necessary (banks may require an audit)

2. ANNUAL REPORT

Within two months after each anniversary date of its incorporation, a company must file an annual report with the Registrar of Companies. The annual report must contain the correct information as of the last anniversary date. The filing fee is $35 (do check this with the Registrar first before filing your report, as this fee may have changed since the publication of this book).

The annual report is a simple form (see Sample 34). The office of the Registrar of Companies in Victoria will automatically send the form to your company's registered office three weeks before your company's anniversary date. The form includes

CONSENT RESOLUTION INSTEAD OF ANNUAL GENERAL MEETING

J & J INDUSTRIES LTD.
(the "Company")

As permitted by Section 140 of the Company Act, we, the undersigned, being all the members of the company, consent in writing to the following resolutions instead of an annual general meeting:

RESOLVED that:

1. Pursuant to Section 179 of the Company Act, the appointment of an auditor for the ensuing year be waived.
2. The presentation of financial statements of the Company for the last fiscal year be waived.

OR

1. The financial statements prepared and approved by the Company's auditor have been presented to each member.
2. All acts, contracts, proceedings, appointments and payments of money by the directors of the Company since the last annual meeting as appear in the proceedings and records of the Company be approved, ratified, and confirmed.
3. The following persons be elected as directors of the Company until the next annual meeting, having received a consent to act in writing from each:
   Jack Doe
   John Doe
   Jean Doe

DATED as of the 1st day of June, 200- by all the members who would have been entitled to attend and vote at the annual general meeting.

John Doe
_____
JOHN DOE

Jack Doe
_____
JACK DOE

SAMPLE 33
DIRECTORS' CONSENT RESOLUTION TO APPOINT OFFICERS

J & J INDUSTRIES LTD.
(the "Company")

According to the Company Act, the following resolutions are passed by the directors of the company, consented to in writing by all the directors of the company:

RESOLVED that the following persons be elected officers of the company until the next annual general meeting:

John Doe President   Jean Doe Vice-President
Jack Doe Secretary/Treasurer

DATED as of the 1st day of June, 200-.

John Doe
_____
JOHN DOE

Jack Doe
_____
JACK DOE

Jean Doe
_____
JEAN DOE

SAMPLE 34
ANNUAL REPORT FORM

BRITISH COLUMBIA

Ministry of Finance
and Corporate Relations
Corporate and Personal
Property Registries

2nd floor – 940 Blanshard Street
PO Box 9431 Stn Prov Govt
Victoria BC V8W 9V3
Telephone: (250) 356-8626
Hours: 8:30 – 4:30 Monday to Friday

ANNUAL REPORT
FORM 16
Sections 333 and 334
COMPANY ACT

Instructions for completion on reverse.
Attach an additional sheet if more space is required.

Filing Fee $35.00   Page 1 of 1

FULL NAME OF COMPANY	CERTIFICATE OF INCORPORATION NUMBER
J & J Industries Ltd.	654321

	YYYY	MM	DD
DATE OF INCORPOR-ATION, AMALGAMATION OR CONTINUATION	200-	06	01

REGISTERED OFFICE ADDRESS

111A Street
Anywhere, BC Z1P 0G0

IS THIS A REPORTING COMPANY?
No

DATE OF ANNUAL REPORT (ANNIVERSARY DATE)	YYYY 200-	MM 06	DD 01

OFFICE USE ONLY – DO NOT WRITE IN THIS AREA

Has there been a change of registered or records office address? If YES, a Notice to Change Office (Form 4) must be filed. See instructions on reverse.

Has there been a change of directors? If YES, a Notice of Directors (Form 8/9) must be filed. See instructions on reverse.

DIRECTORS – List all directors' names and addresses

LAST NAME	FIRST NAME & INITIALS (IF ANY)	RESIDENTIAL ADDRESS	CITY	PROVINCE	POSTAL CODE
Doe	John	111A Street, Anywhere, BC			Z1P 0G0
Doe	Jean	333C Street, Anywhere, BC			Z1P 0G0
Doe	Jack	222B Street, Anywhere, BC			Z1P 0G0

OFFICERS – List all officers' names, addresses and titles

PRESIDENT

Doe	John	111A Street, Anywhere, BC			Z1P 0G0

SECRETARY

Doe	Jack	222B Street, Anywhere, BC			Z1P 0G0

VICE PRESIDENT

DOE	Jean	333C Street, Anywhere, BC			Z1P 0G0

CERTIFIED CORRECT – I have read this form and found it to be correct.
Signature of a current Director, Officer, or Company Solicitor

X

DATE SIGNED		
YYYY	MM	DD

FIN 718/H Rev. 1999 / 7 / 23 (Prescribed)

123

information up to the date of the previous annual report. You should make changes, if any, to bring the report up to date (cross out the old information and add the new information). Don't forget to sign it, then send it in with your filing fee. And ensure you file a copy of the annual report in your minute book.

Section 257 of the Company Act provides that if a company doesn't file an annual report (or any other notice required to be filed) for two years, the Registrar of Companies can have the company struck off the record. This can be serious if the company owns valuable assets like land. If the company isn't in good standing, it cannot sell any land or assets it owns until it becomes reinstated. This is a time-consuming and expensive procedure, because all the missing annual reports must be filed and a court application made to re-register the company. It's therefore far better to keep your filings up to date and avoid these problems.

12
ALL ABOUT MEETINGS

1. GENERAL MEETINGS

If your articles provide for it, or if you're a one-person company, a quorum of one can constitute a meeting (see section 144 of the Company Act). Your meetings must be held within the province, and all members are entitled to receive at least 21 days' notice. Minutes of all meetings and proceedings must be kept and entered in the company's minute book.

Your annual general meeting, if you have one, must be held within 15 months of incorporation, and thereafter no more than 13 months later than the date the last meeting was held. If you decide to waive your annual general meeting by written consent resolution, you must file this in your minute book (see chapter 11 for more information on annual general meetings).

Section 147 allows a shareholder holding one-twentieth or more of the shares to require a general meeting be held by giving written "requisition" notice to the directors stating the purpose for holding this meeting. A general meeting must then be held within four months. There is no restriction on the reasons needed for calling such a meeting, so in most small non-reporting companies, practically any shareholder can legally enforce the calling of a meeting. In practice, however, forced meetings will likely be rare.

2. DIRECTORS' MEETINGS

Under the Company Act, the directors hold virtually total authority for the operation of the company. Therefore, there will likely be numerous occasions when a directors' meeting is necessary.

Directors' meetings must be held in the following circumstances:

(a) When there has been an addition, deletion or substitution of director(s) or shareholder(s)

(b) When a director has an interest in a proposed contract or transaction between the company and another party or company, in which case the director must disclose the nature and extent of his or her interest at the meeting (section 120)

(c) When a director holds any office or possesses property that might create a conflict of interest with his or her position as director, in which case full disclosure is also required (section 123)

(d) When the directors propose to sell, lease or otherwise dispose of a substantial part of, or all of, the undertaking of the company (section 126). A special resolution of shareholders consenting to the transaction is also required (see the discussion in section **3.** on shareholders' meetings).

(e) When the company is repurchasing some of its issued shares

The above items are specifically discussed in the Company Act as requiring some sort of joint director action. In practice, it would probably be wise to call a directors' meeting whenever a matter of substantial business importance arises because of the liability and responsibility of directors.

There is one way in which the directors' business may be conducted without holding these meetings, and that is detailed in section 125 (3), which states as follows:

> 125(3)   Unless the articles provide otherwise, any resolution of the directors or of any committee of them may be passed without a meeting if all the directors, or the members of the committee, as the case may be, consent to the resolution in writing and the consent is filed with the minutes of proceedings of the directors or the committee.

There are no provisions in our model set of articles *requiring* the directors to hold a meeting, so you may dispense with directors' meetings altogether provided the proper resolutions are filed and consented to (see part 15.12 of articles).

A meeting may be very informal. Under section 125(2) of the Company Act, directors may hold meetings by telephone if the articles allow it. Part 15.13 of the articles in Sample 8 allows you to hold meetings by telephone. Just make sure you draw up the proper minutes, have them signed, and file a copy in the minute book.

3.   SHAREHOLDERS' MEETINGS

There are relatively few situations outlined in the Company Act or articles where a shareholders' meeting is a must. However, you would be wise to call a shareholders' meeting whenever you feel directors are getting into "deep water" because of the extent of their personal liability for their actions as directors. Shareholder approval would almost certainly cure any act of the directors on behalf of the company, as long as it was done honestly and in good faith.

Traditionally, shareholders' meetings were restricted to the annual general meeting where, in a private non-reporting company, their function was to approve the actions of the directors for the preceding year. Now, the annual general meeting can be waived by the shareholders, so a shareholders' meeting is not required as a part of the normal operation of the company.

In fact, there is practically no need to hold meetings. Under the Company Act, resolutions or decisions can be made by written agreement. If you hold a meeting to discuss and make business decisions, you must keep minutes of the meeting which must be filed in the company's minute book. If written consent resolutions are used instead, the consent resolutions must be filed in the company's minute book.

Some business decisions can be made by "ordinary resolution." In other cases, a "special resolution" is required.

3.1   Ordinary resolution

An ordinary resolution is a resolution or decision passed by the majority of shareholder votes at a meeting, or if no meeting is held, a decision consented to in writing by shareholders carrying three-quarters or more votes.

Examples of business decisions requiring only an ordinary resolution include the following:

(a)   Appointing a new director to replace a director removed before the end of his or her term

(b)   Removing and replacing an auditor before the expiration of the auditor's term

3.2   Special resolution

A special resolution is a decision passed by three-quarters or more votes of the shareholders who attend a meeting or, if no meeting is held, a unanimous decision consented to in writing by every shareholder.

Special resolutions are required for a number of business acts, including the following:

(a) Altering the articles

(b) Changing the company's name (by altering the memorandum)

(c) Selling or disposing of substantially all of the company's assets

(d) Creating, defining, or attaching special rights or restrictions to shares (by altering the memorandum or articles)

(e) Increasing, decreasing, or changing the authorized share capital (by altering the memorandum)

(f) Amalgamating with another company

(g) Continuing (transferring the company) to another province

(h) Removing a director before the end of his or her term

13
ALL ABOUT DIRECTORS AND OFFICERS

1. HOW MANY DIRECTORS AND OFFICERS DO YOU NEED?

Every non-reporting company needs at least one director. One of your directors must ordinarily be a resident of British Columbia, and a majority of the directors must ordinarily reside in Canada.

You'll need a president and a secretary as officers, who must be different people. If you have a one-person company, you can be both president and secretary at the same time. For all companies, the president must also be a director. Of course, your articles may allow a large number of officers.

2. WHAT CHARACTERISTICS MUST THEY HAVE?

The qualifications for directors are set out in detail in section 114 of the Company Act. Basically, a director must be 18 years old or older. He or she may not be an undischarged bankrupt, a corporation, or a person suffering from mental infirmity.

Also, someone who has been convicted of an offence involving fraud or an offence concerning the promotion, formation, or management of a company must wait five years from the sentence imposed before he or she is eligible to become a director.

The above qualifications also apply to officers.

3. HOW TO APPOINT DIRECTORS AND OFFICERS

With most non-reporting companies, the articles normally provide that all directors must retire at each annual general meeting and new directors are to be elected (see Part 14 of Sample 8). In most cases, however, the old directors are simply appointed to a new term by the consent resolution shown in Sample 32 in chapter 11.

Remember that appointed directors must be present at the meeting at which they are elected or have consented previously to the appointment in writing. Sample 28 shown in chapter 7 is an example of such a consent.

The directors have complete authority to appoint and discharge any officers, unless the articles state otherwise (they rarely do). Remember that the president must also be a director. If your company has two or more shareholders, it must also have at least two officers (a president and secretary).

Unless there is a change of directors, or a subscriber to the memorandum doesn't wish to become a director, you need file no further forms with the Registrar of Companies upon incorporation. However, when a director resigns or is removed from office, or when you appoint or elect a new director, you must file a Notice of Directors with the Registrar of Companies within 14 days. An example is shown in Sample 35.

Other than at the annual general meeting, a special resolution by all the shareholders is needed to remove a director from office (see chapter 12 for more information on special resolutions). Officers may be dismissed by a majority vote of the directors.

SAMPLE 35
NOTICE OF DIRECTORS

BRITISH COLUMBIA

Telephone: (250) 356-8626
Hours: 8:30 – 4:30 (Monday – Friday)

Ministry of Finance and Corporate Relations
Corporate and Personal
Property Registries

Mailing Address:
PO Box 9431 Stn Prov Govt
Victoria BC V8W 9V3
Location:
2nd Floor – 940 Blanshard Street
Victoria BC

NOTICE OF DIRECTORS
Form 8 / 9
Sections 113 and 132 *COMPANY ACT*

INSTRUCTIONS:

1. **Please type or print clearly in block letters and ensure that the form is signed and dated in ink. Complete all areas of the form.** The Registry may have to return documents that do not meet this standard. Attach an additional sheet if more space is required.
2. In Box A, enter the exact name of the company as shown on the Certificate of Incorporation, Amalgamation, Continuation or Change of Name.
3. In Box D, E and F, enter the last name, first name, and any initials of the company's directors as indicated.
4. In Box F, the residential address of a director must be a complete **physical address.** You may include general delivery, post office box, rural route, site or comp. number as part of the address, but the Registry can not accept this information as a complete address. You must also include a postal code. If an area does not have street names or numbers, provide a description that would readily allow a person to locate the director.
5. If changes occurred on more than one date, you must complete a separate Notice of Directors form for each date.
6. An individual who has ceased being a director cannot sign this form.
7. **Filing fee: $20.00.** Submit this form with a cheque or money order payable to the Minister of Finance and Corporate Relations, or provide the Registry authorization to debit the fee from a BC Online Deposit Account.
8. Additional information and forms are available on the internet at: http://www.fin.gov.bc.ca/corppg/default.htm

CERTIFICATE OF INCORPORATION NO.

654321

OFFICE USE ONLY – DO NOT WRITE IN THIS AREA

Freedom of Information and Protection of Privacy Act **(FIPPA):** The personal information requested on this form is made available to the public under the authority of the *Company Act.* Questions about how the *FIPPA* applies to this personal information can be directed to the Administrative Analyst, Corporate and Personal Property Registries at (250) 356-0944, PO Box 9431 Stn Prov Govt, Victoria BC V8W 9V3.

FULL NAME OF COMPANY

J & J Industries Ltd.

DATE OF CHANGE

2 0 0 0 | 0 1 | 2 3 (YYYY MM DD)

Full names of new directors appointed:

LAST NAME	FIRST NAME AND INITIALS *(IF ANY)*
Doe	Jean

Full names of persons who have ceased to be directors:

LAST NAME	FIRST NAME AND INITIALS *(IF ANY)*
Doe	Jack

Full names and addresses of all the directors of the company as at the date of change listed above:

LAST NAME	FIRST NAME AND INITIALS *(IF ANY)*	RESIDENTIAL ADDRESS *(INCLUDE POSTAL/ZIP CODE)*
Doe	John	111A Street, Anywhere, BC Z1P 0G0
Doe	Jean	333C Street, Anywhere, BC Z1P 0G0

CERTIFIED CORRECT – I have read this form and found it to be correct.
Signature of a current Director, Officer, or Company Solicitor

X *John Doe -- President*

DATE SIGNED
2 0 0 - 0 1 2 8 (YYYY MM DD)

FIN 753 Rev. 1999 / 10 / 29 (Prescribed)

4. THE POWERS OF MANAGEMENT

Under the Company Act, the directors must manage, or supervise the management of, the affairs and business of the company in accordance with the company's articles. They are able to do almost anything on behalf of the company. They can, for example, make major changes in the company and make charitable gifts at their own discretion, without seeking shareholder approval.

Technically speaking, the directors are so powerful that it's doubtful whether a majority of shareholders could overrule a decision. Further, as a non-reporting company is empowered to buy and redeem its own shares, there are opportunities for directors to manipulate share values and protect their positions. However, this probably isn't something you should worry about, as in a non-reporting company, the directors and shareholders are nearly always the same people.

Also, there are certain restrictions on the directors' powers. In particular, the directors cannot sell, lease or dispose of all or substantially all of the company's "undertaking" or assets without the shareholders approving this by special resolution (i.e., three-quarters vote at a meeting or unanimous written consent).

Remember that the directors cannot avoid having a meeting (to decide on selling, leasing, or disposing of the assets) among themselves by using a signed resolution, unless they unanimously consent to their resolution (see chapter 12). If any director dissents, he or she will have to call a meeting so that the resolution may be passed by the majority of the directors and the dissent noted by the secretary in the minutes of the meeting.

5. DUTIES AND RESPONSIBILITIES OF DIRECTORS AND OFFICERS

So you are a director. Even though your board meetings are held at the kitchen table, your duties are the same as those of directors who sit around a long teak table surrounded by graphs and plush carpets.

Read this section carefully, together with sections 117 to 123 of the Company Act, so you may fully understand your duties. Even if you're only an officer, like a secretary or treasurer, you'll want to know about directors' duties and responsibilities. The Company Act imposes the same duties and responsibilities on officers that it imposes on directors.

In general, every director and officer must act "honestly and in good faith and in the best interests of the company." You are also required to "exercise the care, diligence and skill of a reasonably prudent person."

5.1 Payment for shares

Directors are prohibited from issuing shares until the company has been fully paid for those shares. The payment may be money, past work or services, or property (like land or machinery). In the case of property or past work or services, the directors may decide the value of such property or past work or service by resolving that, after carefully considering the matter, the property or service was provided to the company at fair market value. It is not possible to issue shares in exchange for someone's promissory note or future services. For full details, see sections 42 and 43 of the Company Act.

5.2 Conflict of interest

How does the Company Act deal with the problems of conflict of interest and the duty to act in the best interests of the company? By making directors and officers disclose to the other directors the nature and extent of the conflict.

Disclosure must be made if —

(a) a director is directly or indirectly interested in a proposed contract or transaction with the company, or

(b) a director holds any office creating a competing duty, or possesses any property giving rise to a competing interest, that causes a conflict with his or her duty as a director to the company.

The disclosure must be made at the first meeting in which the competing contract is discussed (or as soon after holding the competing office or acquiring the competing property).

In the case of a proposed contract or transaction, if a director doesn't promptly disclose the competing interest to the board, the interested director or officer must disclose the interest to the shareholders. The shareholders can then approve the contract by special resolution. The contract, when the company enters into it, must also be fair and reasonable. In some ways, this puts a director or officer in a precarious position — the shareholders may approve the contract, but a court at a later date may decide that the contract wasn't fair and reasonable. A director can, therefore, be left wondering for a long time whether or not he or she is entitled to keep the profit from any contract in which he or she was interested.

As you can see, the duty to disclose is an onerous one. But it *must* be met if a director is to avoid being severely penalized later. The easiest solution is to be very candid with the other directors and to have their acknowledgement recorded in the minutes of the meeting.

Often when you have to disclose a competing contract to the shareholders, the competitors are the other directors. If they approve the contract by special resolution, it will cost a minority shareholder a lot of money to go to court to have the contract set aside on the grounds that it wasn't fair and reasonable at the time it was made.

Finally, even if the interest of a director or officer in a contract is never disclosed, the contract is still valid until the court sets it aside or stops its completion on the application of a shareholder or "some other interested party." The company itself cannot avoid the contract at its own option.

Bear in mind, however, that directors who haven't disclosed a personal interest or profit in a contract made by the company have been treated very severely by the courts. Ultimately, they've lost far more than the profit.

5.3 Personal liability

If you violate the provisions of the Company Act and the company suffers proven loss as a result, you'll be personally liable to make up this loss (see section 127 of the act).

However, you won't be held accountable if you prove that you didn't know and couldn't reasonably have known that the action authorized by the directors' resolution was contrary to the Company Act. You're also entitled to rely and act in good faith upon the company's financial statements presented to you by its officers. Further, if a resolution was passed approving something that goes against the Company Act, and you dissented and had your dissent recorded in writing, you'll also have a strong defence.

Another way you can be held personally liable is as an insider. As an insider with intimate knowledge of the company's affairs, you're liable to compensate anyone (such as a shareholder) who suffers direct loss as a result of a share transaction in which you use confidential information to your benefit — information that, if generally known, could have reasonably affected the value of the shares.

But even if you knowingly break these laws, there is a two-year limitation period imposed on any legal action brought. This may effectively prevent liquidators, trustees in bankruptcy, and shareholders from holding you responsible after two years.

As a director, you should also be aware of the Employment Standards Act, which makes all directors and officers personally liable for the unpaid wages of an employee. You are personally liable for up to two months' wages for each employee who hasn't been paid.

5.4 Liability under the Income Tax Act

If your corporation doesn't deduct and remit income tax from employees' salaries, the directors and the corporation will be jointly liable for the amount that should have been paid, plus interest and penalties. However, any director who has shown a degree of care to prevent the non-payment and remittance of the income tax may not be liable.

If any action is to be taken against a director on this point, it must be started no later than two years after he or she ceased to be a director.

6. YOUR ESCAPE ROUTES

Suppose you do break one of the provisions of the Company Act and are accountable to the company (or to the shareholders under the insider trading provisions). Or, suppose you're guilty of an offence under the act and must pay a fine. What can you do?

(a) You can obtain shareholder approval for the violation to excuse you from your duty to act as a reasonable, prudent person in good faith.

(b) The court may approve and allow the company to indemnify or reimburse you against any liability you face, even if it's the company itself that brings the legal action against you. To be indemnified, however, you must prove you were acting in good faith, honestly, and reasonably. The court must also conclude that you should honestly and reasonably be excused.

To protect yourself as a director or officer from the financial consequences of legal action, the company can buy liability insurance for you. But this insurance isn't cheap and, in the case of a non-reporting company involved in a speculative venture, can be prohibitively expensive.

14
SHAREHOLDER RIGHTS AND REMEDIES

The Company Act gives quite broad rights to shareholders. If you have an unresolved complaint about the company's dealings, you can go to court. There are four main remedies you can pursue:

    (a)   The oppression remedy (section 200)

    (b)   A derivative action (section 201)

    (c)   Dissent proceedings (section 207)

    (d)   Winding-up of the company (section 271)

In most cases, if you wish to pursue one of these remedies, you'll need the help of a lawyer. Sometimes, however, simply having everyone know what a shareholder's rights are may be sufficient to resolve the problem.

1. OPPRESSION REMEDY

The oppression remedy may be chosen when the conduct of the shareholders or directors is oppressive or unfairly prejudicial to one or more shareholders.

Section 200 of the Company Act states that the shareholder or shareholders affected can apply to the court for an oppression remedy if —

    (a)   the affairs of the company, or the powers of the directors, are being exercised in an oppressive manner;

    (b)   some act of the company has been done (or is threatened) that is (or would be) unfairly prejudicial; or

    (c)   some resolution of the members has been passed (or is proposed) that is (or would be) unfairly prejudicial.

For example, if you could show that you were the victim of "share watering" (i.e., when newly issued shares aren't offered to existing shareholders on a pro rata basis), or that you had suffered damages as a minority shareholder because the Company Act hadn't been followed, you may have rights under the oppression remedy. Other examples of oppressive actions include the company's failure to hold an annual general meeting in certain circumstances, failure to provide financial statements, and payment of excessive director and officer fees.

Traditionally, the test of whether an act has been oppressive or unfairly prejudicial has been whether the majority has dealt honestly and fairly with the minority. Bad faith isn't necessarily required — an honest but mistaken act can be oppressive.

You should note that the oppression section is directed to wrongs done to the *shareholder*, not wrongs done to the company.

The types of orders the court can make are set out in section 200(2) of the Company Act and include the following:

    (a)   Prohibiting any act or directing an act be carried out

    (b)   Ordering the company to compensate the affected person

    (c)   Requiring the company to produce its financial statements

    (d)   Directing one shareholder buy the shares of another

(e) Ordering that the company be wound up

This list isn't exhaustive — the court can grant any order it considers appropriate to resolve the complaint.

2. DERIVATIVE ACTION

A derivative action refers to legal proceedings brought by a shareholder or director who stands in the place of the company to sue on behalf of the company, or to defend an action brought against the company. While this is technically referred to as a derivative action, you may hear this type of proceeding referred to as a "class" or "representative" action.

In a derivative action, the action is brought to remedy a wrong against the *company*. In this way, it differs from the oppression remedy, because with the oppression remedy, the action is brought to remedy a wrong against an individual shareholder or group of shareholders.

In most cases, a derivative action is used by a minority shareholder or shareholders who wish to force the directors of the company (who are usually majority shareholders) to do something for the benefit of, or stop doing something that is harmful to, the company and the minority shareholders. (Since it's the company that is supposed to be suffering, in normal circumstances, it would be the company that would take the action. However, the minority, not being in control of the board of directors, cannot get the company to act. Consequently, they can sue only as representatives of the company.)

To start a derivative action, you must apply to court for leave or permission. Section 201(8) of the Company Act says that you must show —

(a) that you've made reasonable efforts to cause the directors of the company to start or defend the action,

(b) that you are acting in good faith,

(c) that, on the face of it, the action is in the best interests of the company, and

(d) that you were a member (shareholder) of the company at the time of the transaction or event giving rise to the cause of the action.

Past cases indicate that a minority shareholder or shareholders may start a derivative action in the following situations:

(a) When the company is doing or intends to do something beyond its powers (this would only apply to companies with restricted objects in the memorandum)

(b) When the company is doing or intends to commit fraud against the minority, and the persons controlling the company's activities will benefit from the fraud

(c) When a resolution has been or is proposed to be passed that needs more than 50% of the voting shares, but is or has been passed by only 50% of the voting shares (split vote)

There may also be other situations where a derivative action can be pursued.

Any money recovered in a successful lawsuit belongs to the company and not to the individual shareholders or director who took the action.

To help with the financing of such a lawsuit, legal costs may be recovered during and after the course of the action by the persons in control of the action.

3. DISSENT PROCEEDINGS BY SHAREHOLDERS

The dissent proceedings remedy is probably the most effective for most shareholders. In short, in certain situations where a minority shareholder disagrees or dissents to a proceeding by the company, the company must purchase his or her shares at fair market value. The parties must agree on fair market value and, if there is no agreement, they can apply to the court to resolve the matter.

Under section 207, the situations where dissent proceedings may be taken are as follows:

(a) On transferring the company to another province

(b) On a sale, lease, or disposition of all or most of the company's assets (except for a mortgage)

(c) If the company gives financial assistance to someone who will then hold 90% of its shares

(d) If the company changes the restrictions on its business or its powers

(e) On converting from a specially limited company (NPL company) to a regular, non-reporting company

(f) On amalgamating with another company

(g) On selling the company's assets to shareholders when the company is being wound up (see section **4.** below for information on winding up a company)

Before initiating dissent proceedings, the shareholder must, however, give the directors the necessary notice within the time stated by the Company Act. These time limits differ, depending on the particular reason for wanting to start dissent proceedings (see section 207).

The broad nature of the right to bring dissent proceedings means that every time a company proposes to pass a special resolution, you, as a director, should automatically consider whether dissent proceedings may be brought into play.

Afterward, once the company has bought the shares, the capital of the company is reduced. In setting the price and terms of the purchase, the court must have "due regard for the rights of creditors." But it's not necessary for real creditors to consent to the reduction of capital.

4. INVOLUNTARY WINDING-UP

The most drastic remedy an aggrieved shareholder has is to ask the court to "wind up" the company, that is, dissolve the company. Under section 271 of the Company Act, the court can order the winding-up of a company when a shareholder, creditor, director, or other interested person applies for it — if the court thinks it just and equitable.

Reasons for winding up a company under the "just and equitable rule" include a deadlock between two equal shareholders who can't agree on how the company should be run and a justifiable lack of confidence in the conduct of the company's affairs.

In addition, if the company's memorandum and articles state that the company may be wound up on the happening of an event, the court may make such an order if the event occurs. This provision allows for the speedy winding-up of a company under the articles, instead of a lawsuit between shareholders as to whether or not the company should be wound up.

Because of the division of legislative responsibility in Canada, an insolvent company in British Columbia must be put into bankruptcy or wound up under the provisions of the federal Winding-up Act.

15
HOW TO CHANGE YOUR COMPANY NAME OR OFFICES

1. CHANGING THE COMPANY NAME

So you've been operating your company for a couple of years now. But you've come to the realization that the name "Slipshod Industries Ltd." wasn't the most brilliant of ideas. Or perhaps the name no longer reflects what you do. Or maybe it's caused you unforeseen problems, such as midnight telephone calls to your home by stranded motorists who track you down through a name like "Marvin Mechanic Towing Services Ltd." Or perhaps "North End Appliance Repairs Inc." is now embarrassing because you've moved to the south end of town.

Whatever the reason, it's possible to change your company name by a fairly simple procedure. Section 223 of the Company Act allows a name change (documented in the memorandum) so long as the shareholders agree to this by special resolution.

You must go through the same reservation procedure and pay the name search and reservation fee as discussed in chapter 4. Then a special resolution to change the company name can be consented to in writing and signed by all the members (see Sample 36). You can now prepare the altered memorandum and attach it to the resolution (see Sample 37).

After obtaining all shareholders' signatures on the special resolution and filing it in the minute book under the shareholder minutes and resolutions, you're ready to prepare a certified copy of the resolution on Form 19 (found at the back of the Company Act under "Schedules") to send to the Registrar of Companies (see Sample 38).

You should send two copies of this Form 19 with the attached memorandum, so you'll receive a stamped copy back for your minute book along with the change of name certificate. A covering letter is shown as Sample 39. A cheque covering the fees and made payable to the Minister of Finance should accompany these documents. (Fees at the time of publication were $100 for the name change and $25 to get back a certified copy of the completed Form 19 with attached altered memorandum.)

One final comment about changing a company name: if you want a catchy name primarily for advertising value, it may be unnecessary for you to go through this process. You can simply adopt a trade name with no forms to fill out as long as your intention is not to steal someone else's name or defraud your creditors in any way.

So, for example, J & J Industries Ltd. could operate as "JJ's Pipe and Pot Shop." Your letterhead and signs would then have to read:

JJ's PIPE AND POT SHOP
owned and operated by
J & J Industries Ltd.

or

JJ's PIPE AND POT SHOP
(a division of)
J & J Industries Ltd.

SAMPLE 36
SPECIAL RESOLUTION TO CHANGE COMPANY NAME

J & J INDUSTRIES LTD.
(the "Company")

We, the undersigned, being all the members of the company, consent in writing to the following special resolutions:

RESOLVED that:

1.   According to section 223 of the Company Act, the name of the company be changed from J & J INDUSTRIES LTD. to JJ's PIPE AND POT SHOP LTD. and that the memorandum be amended accordingly.

2.   The altered memorandum be attached as Schedule "A."

DATED as of the 6th day of July, 200-.

John Doe _____
JOHN DOE

Jack Doe _____
JACK DOE

SAMPLE 37
ALTERED MEMORANDUM

SCHEDULE "A"

Form 1
(Section 5)

COMPANY ACT

ALTERED MEMORANDUM
(as altered by special resolution passed July 6, 200-)

1.   The name of the company is JJ's PIPE AND POT SHOP LTD.

2.   The authorized capital of the company consists of TEN THOUSAND (10 000) Common shares without par value.

137

SAMPLE 38
FORM 19 — SPECIAL RESOLUTION TO CHANGE COMPANY NAME

BRITISH COLUMBIA

Form 19
(Section 348)

Certificate of Incorporation No. _654321_

COMPANY ACT

SPECIAL RESOLUTION

The following special resolution* was passed by the undermentioned company on the date stated:

Name of Company _J & J Industries Ltd._

Date resolution passed _July 6, 200-_

Resolution †

RESOLVED THAT:

1. According to Section 223 of the Company Act, the name of the company be changed from J & J INDUSTRIES LTD. to JJ's PIPE AND POT SHOP LTD. and that the memorandum be amended accordingly.

2. The altered memorandum be attached as Schedule "A".

	YYYY	MM	DD

Certified a true copy on

(Signature) _John Doe_

Director

(Relationship to company)

* *See* section 1 (1) for definition of "special resolution".
† Insert text of special resolution.
R. C. — 14

FIN 766 Rev. 1999 / 2 / 8

138

Registrar of Companies
PO Box 9431
Victoria, BC V8W 9V3

July 7, 200-

Dear Registrar:

Re: J & J INDUSTRIES LTD. #654321

Enclosed please find the following:

1.   Duplicate copies of the Special Resolution to Change the Company's Name

2.   Duplicate copies of altered Memorandum (Schedule "A")

3.   Certified cheque payable to the Minister of Finance for the sum of $125.

We have reserved the name JJ's Pipe and Pot Shop Ltd. under number 63574. Would you kindly process the change of name application and forward to me the change of name certificate.

Thank you for your cooperation.

Yours truly,

John Doe

John Doe

(If you use "a division of," those three words must be in parentheses.) In this way you avoid any problems of being accused of misleading customers or creditors. It's all perfectly legal and may be a simpler method of getting what you want.

2. CHANGING YOUR RECORDS OR REGISTERED OFFICE

If you wish to change the location of your records or registered office, section 40 of the Company Act details the procedure you must follow and the documents you must submit to the Registrar of Companies.

First, prepare a directors' consent resolution, in writing, as shown in Sample 40. After obtaining all directors' signatures on this resolution and filing this in your minute book, prepare a Notice to Change Office (see Sample 41). Then send two signed copies of the Notice to Change Office to the Registrar, along with the appropriate filing fees. The change will only be effective if two copies of the notice have been filed with the Registrar.

If you decide to use a law firm as your company's new registered and records office address, they will prepare the appropriate documents for you.

SAMPLE 40
DIRECTORS' CONSENT RESOLUTION TO CHANGE OFFICES

J & J INDUSTRIES LTD.
(the "Company")

According to the Company Act the following resolutions are passed by the directors of the company, consented to in writing by all the directors of the company:

RESOLVED that the registered and records offices of the company be changed from

123 West First Street
Somewhere, BC V7J 1H1

to

#201 - 600 Main Street
Nowhere, BC V1P 0G0.

DATED as of the 15th day of August, 200-.

John Doe
_____
JOHN DOE

Jack Doe
_____
JACK DOE

SAMPLE 41
NOTICE TO CHANGE OFFICES

BRITISH COLUMBIA

Ministry of Finance
and Corporate Relations
Corporate and Personal
Property Registries
Telephone: (250) 356-8626
Hours: 8:30 – 4:30 (Monday – Friday)

Mailing Address:
PO Box 9431 Stn Prov Govt
Victoria BC V8W 9V3
Location:
2nd Floor – 940 Blanshard Street
Victoria BC

**NOTICE TO
CHANGE OFFICE
(Form 4)**

Section 40 *COMPANY ACT*

INSTRUCTIONS:

1. **Please type or print clearly in block letters and ensure that the form is signed and dated in ink. Complete all areas of the form. The Registry may have to return documents that do not meet this standard.**

2. In Box A, enter the exact name as shown on the Certificate of Incorporation, Amalgamation, Continuation or Change of Name.

3. In Box C and E, enter the addresses currently registered at the Corporate Registry.

4. In Box C, D, E and F, enter the complete **physical address**. You may include general delivery, post office box, rural route, site or comp. number as part of the address, but the Registry cannot accept this information as a complete address. You must also include a postal code. If an area does not have street names or numbers, provide a description that would readily allow a person to locate the office.

   NOTE: A company may locate a registered office and a records office at the same place.

5. If the registered or records office address is that of the solicitor or agent for the company and the solicitor or agent move their place of business, the solicitor or agent must file a new Notice to Change Office (Form 4) with the filing fee. The Notice to Change Office (Form 4) must clearly indicate that it is filed under Section 40(4) of the *Company Act*.

6. Please provide the Registry with a **duplicate copy** of this form. Section 40 of the *Company Act* requires the Registry to send a copy of this form to the previous registered or records office except for a notice filed under Section 40(4).

7. **Filing Fee: $20.00.** Submit this form with a cheque or money order made payable to the Minister of Finance and Corporate Relations, or provide the Registry authorization to debit the fee from your BC Online Deposit Account.

B CERTIFICATE OF INCORPORATION NO.

654321

OFFICE USE ONLY – DO NOT WRITE IN THIS AREA

Freedom of Information and Protection of Privacy Act
The personal information requested on this form is made available to the public under the authority of the *Company Act*. Questions about the collection or use of this information can be directed to the Administrative Analyst, Corporate and Personal Property Registries at (250) 356-0944, PO Box 9431 Stn Prov Govt, Victoria BC V8W 9V3.

A FULL NAME OF COMPANY

J & J Industries Ltd.

REGISTERED OFFICE ADDRESS CHANGE
C *FROM* – PREVIOUS ADDRESS

123 West First Street, Somewhere

	PROVINCE	POSTAL CODE
	BC	Z 1 P 0 G 0

D *TO* – NEW ADDRESS

600 Main Street, Nowhere

	PROVINCE	POSTAL CODE
	BC	Z 1 P 0 G 0

RECORDS OFFICE ADDRESS CHANGE
E *FROM* – PREVIOUS ADDRESS

123 West First Street, Somewhere

	PROVINCE	POSTAL CODE
	BC	Z 1 P 0 G 0

F *TO* – NEW ADDRESS

600 Main Street, Nowhere

	PROVINCE	POSTAL CODE
	BC	Z 1 P 0 G 0

G **CERTIFIED CORRECT** – I have read this form and found it to be correct.
Signature of a current Director, Officer, or Company Solicitor

X *John Doe*

DATE SIGNED
Y	M	D
2 0 0 - 0 8		20

Do not separate this form. Return both copies to the Corporate and Personal Property Registries.

FIN 724 Rev. 97 / 5 / 16 (Prescribed)   **WHITE/CANARY:** CORPORATE AND PERSONAL PROPERTY REGISTRIES

16
HOW TO DISSOLVE YOUR COMPANY

Eventually, you may decide that it's no longer worthwhile for you to continue doing business as a company. Perhaps you and the other directors wish to retire, or perhaps substantially all of the company's assets and inventory have been sold. If you want to dissolve your company, you can use the procedure set out in section 258 of the Company Act. This procedure is tailor-made for small, non-reporting companies.

Basically, section 258 allows the Registrar of Companies to dissolve a company (by striking it from the register) if —

    (a)   the company passes an ordinary resolution to have the company struck from the register, and

    (b)   two or more directors of the company (or the sole director, if there's only one director) file an affidavit proving how the company disposed of its assets and stating that the company has no debts or liabilities.

1. BRING YOUR COMPANY UP TO DATE

The Registrar of Companies can refuse to accept any documents (such as a request to strike a company off the register) if a company is behind with its filings. So the first thing you must therefore do is bring your company up to date with the Registrar by making up all unfiled annual reports and other notices. You'll have to pay all the appropriate filing fees for filing these overdue documents.

Next, pay off the creditors of the company, or else get written waivers of their claims. Don't forget that if you loaned money to the company or transferred assets to it in exchange for a promissory note, you are a creditor of the company and are personally entitled to be paid for this debt.

As a shareholder, you're also entitled to share in any of the assets or money remaining after paying off or discharging all of the company's debts, on the basis of the number of issued shares you hold in the company.

2. PASS A RESOLUTION

The next thing you must do is have the shareholders pass an ordinary resolution, either at a specially called meeting or in writing, requesting the Registrar to strike the company off the register (see Sample 42). Then copy or prepare a Form 18 from the back of the Company Act and copy the information from the ordinary resolution onto the form. Have it signed and dated by a director (see Sample 43). This will be the copy you send to the Registrar.

If the company has any assets to be distributed, however, you'll need to pass a special resolution instead of an ordinary resolution (see Sample 44). A special resolution, by definition, is also an ordinary resolution, but because of section 126, you need a special resolution if the company still has assets. Then copy this information onto a Form 19 (see Sample 45).

SAMPLE 42
ORDINARY RESOLUTION TO DISSOLVE A COMPANY

J & J INDUSTRIES LTD.
(the "Company")

We, the undersigned, being all the members of the company, consent in writing to the following resolutions:

WHEREAS:

A. The company wishes to be dissolved under Section 258 of the Company Act.

RESOLVED that:

1. The Registrar of Companies for the Province of British Columbia be requested to strike the company off the Register.

OR

WHEREAS:

A. The company has sold all of its assets to John Doe, 111A Street, Anywhere, BC in consideration for the reduction of the amount owing by the company to John Doe.

B. The company does not carry on any business, and

C. The company has no liabilities to any creditors, except $400 due and owing to Heather Doe of 444D Street, Anywhere, BC which amount Heather Doe has agreed to forgive and forget.

D. It is considered advisable to cause the company to be dissolved under Section 258 of the Company Act.

RESOLVED that:

1. The documents to be filed with the Registrar of Companies under Section 258 of the Company Act be filed, as and when appropriate, requesting the Registrar to strike the company from the register.

DATED this 9th day of July, 200-.

_John Doe_____
JOHN DOE

_Jack Doe_____
JACK DOE

_Jean Doe_____
JEAN DOE

143

SAMPLE 43
FORM 18 — ORDINARY RESOLUTION TO DISSOLVE A COMPANY

BRITISH COLUMBIA

Form 18

(Section 348)

Certificate of
Incorporation No.   654321

COMPANY ACT

ORDINARY RESOLUTION

The following ordinary resolution * was passed by the undermentioned company on the date stated:

Name of company   J & J INDUSTRIES LTD.

Date resolution passed   June 15, 200-

Resolution +

RESOLVED THAT:
1. The Registrar of Companies for the Province of British Columbia be requested to strike the Company off the register.

Certified a true copy on   YYYY   MM   DD

John Doe
_____
(Signature)

Director
_____
(Relationship to Company)

* See section 1 (1) for definition of "ordinary resolution".
\+ Insert text of ordinary resolution.

FIN 778 Rev. 1999 / 3 / 10

J & J INDUSTRIES LTD.
(the "Company")

We, the undersigned, being all the members of the company, consent in writing to the following resolutions:

WHEREAS:

A. The company wishes to be dissolved under Section 258 of the Company Act.

RESOLVED that:

1. The Registrar of Companies for the Province of British Columbia be requested to strike the company off the Register.

2. The property of J & J INDUSTRIES LTD., if any, be distributed rateably among the members of the company according to their rights and interest in the company.

DATED this 9th day of July 200-

John Doe
JOHN DOE

Jack Doe
JACK DOE

Jean Doe
JEAN DOE

BRITISH COLUMBIA

Form 19
(Section 348)

Certificate of Incorporation No. _____654321_____

COMPANY ACT

SPECIAL RESOLUTION

The following special resolution* was passed by the undermentioned company on the date stated:

Name of Company _____J & J Industries Ltd._____

Date resolution passed _____July 6, 200-_____

Resolution †

RESOLVED THAT:

1. The Registrar of Companies for the Province of British Columbia be requested to strike the Company off the Register.

2. The property of J & J INDUSTRIES LTD., if any, be distributed rateably among the Members of the Company according to their rights and interests in the Company.

	YYYY	MM	DD

Certified a true copy on

(Signature) _____*John Doe*_____

_____Director_____

(Relationship to company)

* *See* section 1 (1) for definition of "special resolution".

† Insert text of special resolution.

R. C. — 14

FIN 766 Rev. 1999 / 2 / 8

3. SWEAR THE AFFIDAVIT

The third step in the process is for two directors (or the sole director, if you have a one-person company) to each swear an affidavit stating how the assets have been distributed and that there are no debts or liabilities owing by the company.

Use Sample 46 as a guide. You may alter the body of the affidavit to fit your particular circumstances, but you must keep the words "The Company has no debts or liabilities" in paragraph 4 of Sample 46 exactly as stated.

To ensure there are, in fact, no debts or liabilities of any kind, you should check into the following matters:

(a) Review the company's financial statements.

(b) Review all banking records.

(c) See if any lawsuits remain outstanding or are threatened.

(d) Ensure no taxes are owed to the Canada Customs and Revenue Agency (formerly Revenue Canada).

(e) Confirm all contracts and leases have been concluded or finished.

(f) Ensure the company has no outstanding warranties or guarantees of another's debt.

Once you've prepared the affidavit, the director or directors will have to swear the affidavit before a Commissioner of Oaths. The Commissioner can also certify that the copy of your ordinary or special resolution is a true copy.

4. SUBMIT DOCUMENTS TO THE REGISTRAR

Now mail in your affidavit and the certified copy of the resolution (plus copies of each of these documents) to the Registrar of Companies, together with a cheque to cover the filing fees ($40 at the time of publication of this book). If you still have the certificate of incorporation, you should surrender that too and enclose it with your documents. You should also send a covering letter like the one in Sample 47 with your forms to make sure no confusion arises.

5. STRIKE THE COMPANY OFF THE REGISTER

If all your forms are in order, the Registrar will strike the company from the register and publish a notice to this effect in the *British Columbia Gazette*. You'll also receive a letter from the Registrar confirming the dissolution of your company.

Remember that a company may also be struck off the register involuntarily, for example, if it fails to file annual reports for two consecutive years. If you let your company die this slow death — rather than choosing to dissolve your company under section 258 — valuable assets may be left in the name of the company. It will then be very difficult to transfer them to a creditor or purchaser without going through an expensive reinstatement process. And if you don't reinstate your company, the assets will be forfeited to the provincial government.

The government rarely takes immediate possession of such an asset, as it usually waits for years before taking any action upon this right. However, it's most inconvenient to suddenly, for example, decide you want to sell that piece of land registered in the name of your holding company when the company has been struck off the register. For this reason it's best to properly dissolve your company by resolution and disperse the assets so that there are no loose ends that can come back to haunt you.

AFFIDAVIT

I, John Doe, of 111A Street, Anywhere, BC, V1P 0G0, MAKE OATH AND SAY AS FOL-LOWS:

1. I am the sole director of J & J Industries Ltd. (the "Company"), and as such have personal knowledge of the facts deposed to in this affidavit.

2. The Company has executed an instrument transferring all of its remaining assets, if any, to the sole shareholder [or, to all the shareholders] of the Company,

3. Following the transfer of assets pursuant to the instrument referred to above, the Company has no assets of any kind.

4. The Company has no debts or liabilities.

5. I make this affidavit in support of an application by the Company to the Registrar of Companies of British Columbia to strike the Company off the Register of Com-panies and thereby to effect the dissolution of the Company.

SWORN BEFORE ME at
[location], British Columbia,
on [month, day, year]

}

_____
A Commissioner for taking
Affidavits for British Columbia

John Doe
_____
[name of director]

John Doe,
111 A Street
Anywhere, BC V1P 0G0

December 6, 200-

Registrar of Companies
PO Box 9431
Victoria, BC V8W 9V3

Dear Registrar:

Re: <u>Dissolution of J & J Industries Ltd. #654321</u>

I enclose the following documents (in duplicate) with respect to the dissolution of the above-named company under Section 258 of the Company Act:

1.   Certified copy of the Ordinary Resolution requesting you to strike the company off the register.

2.   Affidavits of John Doe and Jack Doe, directors of the company.

3.   Certificate of Incorporation No.654321.

4.   Cheque in the amount of $40.

   Would you kindly attend to the striking off of the company, file one copy of each document and mail the second filed copy of each document to me at the above address, and mail the confirming memorandum also to the above address.

Yours truly,

John Doe
John Doe

APPENDIX
CHECKLIST OF STEPS TO BE FOLLOWED

_____ Choose name

_____ File Name Approval Request Form along with fee

_____ Order package of incorporation forms or prepare forms

_____ Prepare Memorandum

_____ Prepare Articles

_____ Prepare Notice of Offices

_____ Forward documents to Registrar

    1. Two original signed copies each of Memorandum and Articles

    2. Two original signed copies of Notice of Offices

    3. Cheque payable to Minister of Finance for incorporation fees

_____ Get certified copies of incorporation documents back from Registrar

_____ Buy minute book

_____ Order company seal (optional)

_____ Complete banking resolutions and open bank account

_____ Prepare and sign minutes of various minutes or consent resolutions

    1. Resolutions of Subscribers to Memorandum

    2. Resolutions of Directors

_____ File Notice of Directors (if applicable)

_____ Issue share certificates

_____ Open minute book and insert originals of minutes and copies of all other documents in chronological order

_____ Attend to miscellaneous steps

    1. Transfer assets to company by drafting minutes

    2. Contact Social Services Tax department for exemption form

    3. If motor vehicle involved, contact Motor Vehicle Branch for transfer purposes

_____ File Annual Report